EDITOR: MARTIN WINDROW

OSPREY MILITARY — MEN-AT-ARMS SERIES — 97

MARLBOROUGH'S ARMY 1702-11

Text by
MICHAEL BARTHORP
Colour plates by
ANGUS McBRIDE

Published in 1980 by
Osprey Publishing Ltd
59 Grosvenor Street, London W1X 9DA
© Copyright 1980 Osprey Publishing Ltd
Reprinted 1988, 1989, 1990, 1992

ISBN 0 85045 346 1

Filmset in Great Britain
Printed in Hong Kong

Acknowledgements:
The author is grateful for the assistance given in
various ways by the Marquess of Anglesey, Mr G. A.
Embleton and Mr R. J. Marrion; Messrs Christie's
Limited, the Courtauld Institute of Art, the
National Army Museum, the Scottish United
Services Museum and the Victoria and Albert
Museum. For information about foreign armies he is
indebted to Dr F. Herrmann of Bonn, Dr J. G.
Kerkhoven of the *Koninklijk Nederlands Leger en
Wapenmuseum* of Leyden, and Inga Fl. Rasmussen of
the *Tojhusmuseet*, Copenhagen.

Recommended Further Reading:
The following books should be readily obtainable:
Barnett, Corelli, *Marlborough* (1974)
Chandler, David, *Marlborough as Military Commander*
(1973)
Chandler, David, *The Art of War in the Age of
Marlborough* (1976)
Churchill, Sir Winston S., *Marlborough, His Life and
Times*, 4 vols., (1933) (paperback 1967)
Green, David, *Blenheim* (1974)
Scouller, R. E., *The Armies of Queen Anne* (1966)
Verney, Peter, *The Battle of Blenheim* (1976)
Wace, Alan, *The Marlborough Tapestries at Blenheim
Palace* (1968)

Chronology of the War of the Spanish Succession

1700 The French Duke of Anjou succeeds to the Spanish throne.

1701 February: Louis XIV of France occupies frontier fortresses in the Spanish Netherlands.
June: Earl of Marlborough appointed Captain-General of the English Army and Ambassador-Extraordinary to the Dutch Republic.
September: The Grand Alliance formed against Louis XIV.

1702 March: Queen Anne succeeds William III in England and confirms Marlborough's appointment.
May: Grand Alliance declares war on France.
June: Marlborough recognized as *de facto* Allied Generalissimo by Dutch.

1702–03 Inconclusive campaigns in Low Countries.

1704 19 May: Marlborough's army begins march from Low Countries to join Austrians on the Danube.
22 June: Marlborough links up with Austrians.
2 July: Allies drive Franco-Bavarians from the Schellenberg at Donauworth.
13 August: Battle of Blenheim. Marlborough and Prince Eugene defeat Franco-Bavarians under Marshal Tallard.
November–December: Marlborough's army returns to Low Countries.

1705 May: Allied campaign begins in Netherlands.

17–18 July: Marlborough forces the Lines of Brabant. Battle of Elixem.
September: Lord Peterborough leads expedition to Spain.

1706 May: French advance east out of Spanish Netherlands.
23 May: Battle of Ramillies. Marlborough defeats Marshal Villeroi.
June–October: Marlborough captures all fortresses of Spanish Netherlands between the Meuse and the sea.
Allies in Spain capture Valencia and Madrid, but forced to withdraw.

1707 25 April: Allies in Spain defeated at Almanza.
May–August: Marlborough's Flanders campaign halted by a wet summer.

The Duke of Marlborough. Painting by J. Closterman. (National Army Museum)

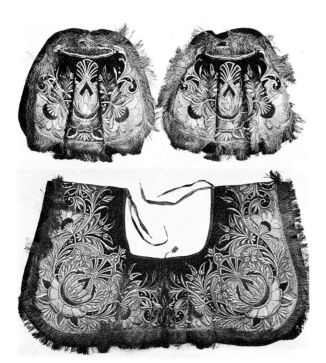

The Duke of Marlborough's horse furniture. *Top:* The holster covers. *Bottom:* The housing. (The London Museum)

1708   June: French in Flanders advance north from Mons.

11 July: Battle of Oudenarde. Marlborough and Prince Eugene defeat Duke of Burgundy and Marshal Vendôme.

August: Marlborough and Prince Eugene begin siege of Lille.

28 September: General Webb defeats French at Wynendael.

9 December: Marshal Boufflers surrenders at Lille.

Allies capture Sardinia and Minorca.

1709   French remain on defensive in Flanders.

July–September: Marlborough besieges and captures Tournai and advances on Mons.

11 September: Battle of Malplaquet. Marlborough and Prince Eugene defeat Marshals Villars and Boufflers, but at heavy cost.

October: Capture of Mons.

Allied operations in Spain continue on Portuguese frontier.

1710   April–November: Marlborough besieges French frontier fortresses on rivers Lys and Scarpe.

Intrigues against Marlborough in England.

In Spain, early Allied successes followed by reverses.

Winter: Marshal Villars begins construction of Lines of '*Ne Plus Ultra*' from Namur, through Arras to the Channel coast.

1711   5 August: Marlborough breaches the Lines at Arleux.

9 August–14 September: Marlborough besieges and captures fortress of Bouchain.

31 December: Political intrigues in England lead to Marlborough's dismissal.

1712   January: Duke of Ormonde takes over Allied army.

July: British troops withdrawn from Flanders.

October: England begins peace negotiations with France.

1713   11 April: Peace of Utrecht.

Political and Military Background

The War of the Spanish Succession represented the second round of the great struggle begun in 1689 by King William III of England to maintain a workable balance of power in Europe by containing the ambitions and lust for glory of King Louis XIV of France. The latter was bent on destroying the United Provinces, as Holland was then known, from which the Protestant William, Prince of Orange, had been summoned in 1688 to replace his Catholic father-in-law, James II, on the English throne. England under James had been in alliance with France but, with the Protestant succession restored, and with James seeking sanctuary with Louis XIV, England's determination to prevent any return of her former monarch coincided with her new Dutch king's resolve to defend the United Provinces. The first round against Louis, therefore, had been fought in the Low Countries by the English and Dutch, together with sundry allies, under the overall command of William III, culminating in the successful capture of the fortress of Namur in 1695, followed two years later by the Peace of Ryswick.

After the death of the childless and demented Charles II of Spain in 1700, his throne, and the Spanish possessions in the Low Countries (now Belgium), Italy and the Americas passed to the grandson of Louis XIV, Philip, Duke of Anjou, thus, in Louis's eyes, effectively uniting France and Spain. Furthermore, Philip's accession ruled out the other claimant to the Spanish throne, the Archduke Charles, younger son of the Hapsburg Emperor Leopold, whose domains of the Holy Roman Empire embraced Austria and most of central Europe. Louis was therefore spared any extension of the Hapsburg influence into Spain and the Spanish Netherlands. But his acceptance of his grandson's accession incurred the hostility of the Emperor, his occupation of the fortresses in the Spanish Netherlands again threatened the United Provinces; while his proclamation of the exiled James II's son as the rightful King of England ensured that country's animosity. Thus in his eagerness to unite the power of Spain with that of France, he provoked the formation of a Grand Alliance between England, Holland and the Empire.

William III despatched John Churchill, Earl of Marlborough, with twelve English battalions to Holland with orders to finalize the war preparations of the Alliance, which was joined by the Electorate of Brandenburg, then in process of becoming the Kingdom of Prussia through an agreement made with the Emperor. William died in 1702 and the whole of the diplomatic and military negotiations to prepare the Alliance for war fell upon Marlborough, who was created Duke by Queen Anne later that year. Austria was menaced by France and her ally, Bavaria, so Marlborough had the task of supplementing his Anglo-Dutch forces with contingents from Prussia, Denmark and various German principalities such as Hanover, Hesse and other minor states. In these negotiations he proved as able in diplomacy as he was soon to prove in generalship. Not until the Blenheim campaign of 1704 did Marlborough's Flanders army unite with the Austrians, and Marlborough himself begin his great partnership with the ablest of the Imperial generals, Prince Eugene of Savoy, which was to prove such a decisive factor in the ensuing years of the war.

Although his British regiments formed a vital component of the army Marlborough led to successive victories between 1704 and 1711—so vital that after Blenheim the French commanders always took special note of where they were deployed in the order of battle—their numbers were relatively small. At Blenheim, for example, out of the Allies' 65 battalions of infantry and 160 squadrons of cavalry, only fourteen and nineteen respectively were British. Marlborough's army was thus very much an international force

A scene of late 17th/early 18th century warfare showing troops in camp. Note the sutler's tent on the left. A tapestry by De Vos from De Hondt's *Art of War*. (Victoria and Albert Museum)

The Storming of the Schellenberg at Donauwörth—detail. Note Marlborough on the right with one of his running footmen, and the dragoons riding forward with fascines across their saddles. One of the tapestries by De Vos after De Hondt at Blenheim Palace. (The Duke of Marlborough)

containing Dutch, Danes, Prussians, Austrians and other Germans, and Marlborough himself was as much an international commander as any NATO general of today. The number of British troops available to him was also reduced by the Government's decision to send a sizeable British force to Spain to co-operate with further Dutch and Portuguese troops in support of the Hapsburg claimant, the Archduke Charles. Although Gibraltar was seized and held for the British Crown in the course of these operations, they never achieved the signal successes won in northern Europe. Had Marlborough had the services of these troops under his command, not to mention others which were removed for operations in the New World, his far-sighted strategic plans for an invasion of France itself, so often baulked by the timidity and prevarication of his allies, might well have been accomplished. (See later table comparing British strengths in Flanders and Spain.)

Warfare in the early 18th century was a formalized affair, bound by a number of conventions and limitations accepted by and applicable to both sides. The primitive nature and scarcity of road and water communications, the immense problems of feeding large numbers of men and horses, aggravated by the shortage of fodder and inadequate facilities for food storage, necessarily

confined the campaigning season to the summer months. From October the contending armies would usually retire into winter quarters until, with the coming of spring, preparations for the next year's campaign began, in particular the amassing of edible and other supplies in magazines and depots. Once an army marched, its rate of movement and range of operations were almost entirely dictated by logistic considerations: the time taken to move forward the supply convoys in its wake and to cut forage for the horses; the provision of sufficient transport, not only for the supplies but for the quantities of fuel and bricks required for the field ovens; and the need to halt every fourth day for rest and resupply. Out of every 100 days an army spent in the field, some 70 would be taken up by logistic arrangements, leaving only 30 for actual operations. Wherever possible pre-stocked magazines were set up along an army's projected line of advance, but unless this lay through friendly territory such supply dumps, and the communications between them and the army, were vulnerable to enemy raids from their fortresses. Most of the campaigns took place either in the Low Countries or northern Italy, areas which by virtue of their relative fertility, prosperity and quality of communications could support field armies, and which occupied strategically important areas on the approaches to France, Holland, North Germany and Austria. Because of their importance, such areas abounded in fortified towns; in view of the vulnerability of an advancing army's supply arrangements, these could not simply be by-passed but had to be reduced by time- and man-power-consuming siege operations, or at least masked, all further diminishing an army's range of operations and capacity for decisive action.

Lastly, the memory of the appalling savagery and devastation wreaked during the Thirty Years War, plus the ever-increasing cost of maintaining standing armies, had bred a more humanitarian approach to war, allied to a reluctance to hazard unduly the expensive forces. All these factors, therefore, tended to produce a leisurely form of war, with long periods for rest and recuperation and a preference for elaborate manoeuvres and sieges conducted according to the agreed conventions, rather than bloody and decisive confrontations on the field of battle. Only commanders of the calibre of Marlborough and Eugene perceived that to win a war, the enemy had to be crushed in battle, then pursued and harassed beyond endurance, thus breaking his will to resist—an aim for which the sieges and manoeuvres were merely means to an end, not an end in themselves. However, they were as much hampered in their resolve by the limitations discussed above as any other commanders, and unless a convincing victory could be fought and won early in the campaigning season, the onset of the autumn rains could allow a beaten enemy time to recuperate for the next year's campaign; a battlefield triumph in, say, August could still result in an indecisive campaign. Only in 1706, with Ramillies won in May, had Marlborough time enough to follow up his victory by clearing the French from almost the whole of the Spanish Netherlands before incessant rain brought the campaign to a close in October. That he was unable to deliver the *coup de grâce* the following year was due to lack of co-operation from his allies and consistently bad weather throughout the summer.

Officers and Men

After the Peace of Ryswick the English Parliament demanded of King William that the Army be reduced to 7,000 troops for England, 12,000 for Ireland and some 4,000 for Scotland. Thus through Parliamentary niggardliness William's battle-tested army of some 50,000 men was reduced by over a half. The regiments that remained, all on low establishments of about 250 for cavalry and 450 for infantry, totalled five troops of Household Cavalry; nine regiments of Horse; eight of Dragoons; three of Foot Guards; and 30 of Foot.

Three years later, with Louis XIV again threatening the peace of Europe, the short-sightedness of Parliament found it out, and all the work to build up an army fit for war had to be done over again. The establishments of existing regiments had to be doubled, and new ones formed. During the course of the war 50 new regiments of

Austrian infantry: musketeer and officer. Light grey coats, faced light blue. The officer has a light blue waistcoat, mixed black-and-gold sash and gold lace on the cuffs. The soldier's belts are buff. Painting by R. Ottenfeld. (Victoria and Albert Museum. Photo: R. J. Marrion)

Austrian infantry: grenadier and drummer. Uniforms are light grey with brass buttons, deep maroon cuffs, red neckcloths and stockings. The grenadier's fur cap has a red bag trimmed with white and a brass plate in front. The drum hoops are red and white, the shell has yellow and black flames with a black eagle on the front. Painting by R. Ottenfeld. (Victoria and Albert Museum. Photo: R. J. Marrion)

Foot, including marines, and seven new cavalry regiments were raised. The greatest strength reached by the Army during the War of the Spanish Succession was 70,000 men at home and abroad, divided between six troops of Household Cavalry, eleven regiments of Horse, sixteen of Dragoons and 79 battalions of Foot. Between 1702 and 1712 the British troops under Marlborough in Flanders averaged just under 22,000, while those in Spain rose from 8,000 in 1704 to 26,000 in 1709.

Such an expansion in an age when conscription was unknown caused the drums of the recruiting parties to beat with renewed vigour through the towns and villages of the British Isles. Many of the ex-soldiers discharged into poverty and neglect after King William's war came forward to rejoin, and there were always a number of adventurous spirits who would take the shilling in search of fame, advancement or simply plunder. Among them were men of some education, like Sergeant Millner of the Royal Irish, John Deane of the 1st

Guards, and Matthew Bishop of Webb's, who all wrote accounts of their experiences. Lack of work in the winter drove many to enlist, while others fell victim to the blandishments and bounty of the recruiting sergeants. However, such men formed the minority and, to find the large numbers required, other methods had to be resorted to: capital offenders were offered enlistment as an alternative to the gallows; vagrants and unemployed were impressed; debtors could obtain release from prison if they enlisted or found a substitute. Since many men were reluctant to enlist for life, as was then the practice, a short-term engagement of only three years with the Colours was introduced, which somewhat eased the recruiting problem. Some regiments were raised entirely from French Huguenots.

Such a diverse, often criminal, and usually unwilling soldiery seemed unpromising material with which to confront Louis XIV's legions, and many could only be kept to their duty by the fear of the lash and the gallows. On the other hand all, whether English, Scots or Irish and whatever their backgrounds, were confident of their superiority over any foreigner. But above all it was Marlborough's inspiring leadership, his building-up of their self-esteem by success in battle, and his concern for their individual well-being by meticulous planning and administration, that welded them together into, if not the largest, certainly the most formidable army in Europe. As Corporal Bishop recorded: 'The Duke of Marlborough's attention and care was over all of us.'

Marlborough's regimental officers were of varied quality. In an age when commissions were bought and sold and a regiment was virtually its colonel's private property, there were many who looked upon their commands as a source of income; others who knew little and cared less about how their regiments should be conducted; and yet others who felt they could come and go as they pleased. Nevertheless, for every gilded popinjay there were serious and dedicated officers like William Kane and Robert Parker, both of the Royal Irish, or the dour Covenanter, John Blackadder of the Cameronians. Though the former type might neglect their duties on the march or in quarters, most regimental officers would lead with gallantry and honour on the battlefield.

To help fulfil his weighty diplomatic and military responsibilities, among which the handling of Allied governments, generals and armies required all his great powers of tact and persuasion, Marlborough chose his staff and subordinates with wisdom and care. Chief among them was his outstanding Quartermaster-General, William Cadogan, who at Oudenarde proved himself as stalwart a field commander as he was able and far-sighted a staff officer. The generals included such competent and experienced men as Lord Orkney, Marlborough's brother Charles Churchill, and Lord Cutts, known as the 'Salamander' for his imperturbability under the hottest fire. Among the lower commanders were the likes of the stout-hearted Brigadier Row, who led the attack on Blenheim village on foot, forbidding his infantry to fire until he had thrust his sword into the French palisades, falling mortally wounded as he did so; Withers, who timed his flank march at Malplaquet to burst in at precisely the right moment on the French left; and Webb, who secured the safe passage of a convoy bearing ammunition for the siege of Lille by beating off a French attack at Wynendael though outnumbered by three to one. Marlborough was well served, too, by his chief artillery officer, Holcroft Blood, and his senior engineer, Colonel Armstrong.

Marlborough (centre) receiving Marshal Tallard escorted by Hessian cavalry after Blenheim. An English infantryman with captured colours is on the right and a grenadier is making off with looted clothing behind Marlborough's staff. After Laguerre. (Courtauld Institute of Art)

Of the senior Allied commanders, the rapport Marlborough established with Prince Eugene was almost telepathic and their brilliantly successful partnership at Blenheim, Oudenarde and Malplaquet must make them one of the most outstanding military combinations of history. The Dutch had a number of capable generals like Ginkel, Goor and the great engineer Coehoorn; but only with Overkirk was Marlborough able to develop something of the mutual trust he enjoyed with Eugene. Marlborough's skill and patience with his allied generals was attested by one of the great figures of the Prussian army, the Prince of Anhalt-Dessau, who, having furiously protested to the Duke about some order, afterwards said: 'The ascendancy of that man is inconceivable. I was unable to utter an angry word; he totally disarmed me in an instant.'

Organization, Armament and Employment

Until the Act of Union between the thrones of England and Scotland in 1707, Queen Anne had an English and a Scottish army. Regiments from both naturally served the Crown in foreign wars, but there was no truly British army until after 1707. For ease of reference, however, it will be spoken of as such hereafter. The remarks that

Godfrey's Regiment charging at Ramillies. A somewhat unreliable reconstruction by R. Simkin. (National Army Museum)

follow refer mainly to British troops, but passing observations will be made on the Allied contingents with whom they operated.

At the head of the Queen's armies stood the Troops of Life or Horse Guards and Horse Grenadier Guards (all now the Life Guards). As the Sovereign's bodyguard they took the field when the Sovereign did so and consequently, since William III had commanded his armies in person, they had fought in his campaigns up to 1697. However, under Anne they remained at home during the War of the Spanish Succession and will therefore not be considered further. The other regiment of today's Household Cavalry, the Blues and Royals, formerly the Royal Horse Guards, was in 1700 the 1st Regiment of Horse, but did not participate in the war.

Cavalry

Cavalry in the early 18th century was of two types —'Horse' and 'Dragoons'—although a third type, of light horsemen, was beginning to make its appearance in some armies. The nine British regiments of Horse (known from 1746 as Dragoon Guards) were numbered in seniority but were usually known by their current colonel's name, and were the most expensive troops in the Army. Each regiment's headquarters would have a colonel, who could well be a general in the Army, a lieutenant-colonel, major, adjutant, chaplain, surgeon and a kettle-drummer. In wartime it would normally consist of nine troops, grouped by threes into a squadron for action; each troop having a captain, lieutenant, cornet, quartermaster, two or three corporals of horse (sergeants),

a trumpeter and between 40 and 60 troopers. The Austrian Horse adopted a twelve-company organization, two of which doubled up to form a squadron. Horse were armed with a straight sword, a brace of pistols, and for the troopers sometimes a carbine as well. Some foreign armies, notably the Dutch, Danish and Austrian, as well as the French and Bavarian, favoured armoured horsemen with back-and-breast cuirasses and, in the case of Austria and Bavaria, the old iron helmets much used in the Thirty Years War and the English Civil War. The British Horse began the war without armour, but after 1707 Marlborough reintroduced the breast plate only, worn under the coat.

The prime task of the Horse on the battlefield was to defeat the enemy cavalry and then fall upon his Foot, guns and baggage. There were two schools of thought as to how this should be done, both stemming from the wars of the previous century: one relied on firepower, delivered by successive ranks of horsemen firing their pistols or carbines at close range and then retiring to reload, all movement being carried out at a steady trot; the other, for which Gustavus Adolphus, Prince Rupert and Cromwell can variously take credit, was based on shock action with the sword. By the early 18th century the French Horse had adopted a compromise—trotting forward to within pistol range, all three ranks of a squadron firing simultaneously, and then falling on with the sword. However, the pause to fire lost the momentum of the advance. The Austrians tended to favour a similar method. Marlborough, on the other hand, trained his Anglo-Dutch squadrons in the true cavalry charge with cold steel, but delivered, not at a gallop or even a canter, but at a fast trot with his squadrons knee-to-knee in two ranks, the momentum and weight of the charge being sustained by the reserve squadrons. So little faith had he in cavalry firepower that he restricted his troopers to three rounds of ammunition, for use when guarding their horses at grass!

Dragoons were defined in the 'Military Dictionary' of 1702 as 'Musketeers mounted, who serve sometimes a-foot, and sometimes a-horseback, being always ready upon anything that requires expedition, as being able to keep pace with the horse, and do the service of the foot.'

They were indeed the handymen of an army, being used for reconnaissances, outposts, escorts, and as what might be termed today assault engineers—clearing obstacles, filling in trenches and demolishing fortifications that would impede the general advance. Nevertheless, despite all these useful functions, they were increasingly being employed as conventional cavalry. Their versatility was demonstrated at the storming of the Schellenberg by Hay's Dragoons (later Royal Scots Greys), who rode forward to drop fascines into ditches so as to facilitate the advance of the Foot, then attacked dismounted as infantrymen and finally, when the enemy broke, remounted and joined in the pursuit.

British dragoon regiments were organized similarly to the Horse but usually had eight troops formed for action into two squadrons. Foreign dragoon regiments tended to be somewhat larger than their Horse. The dragoon was armed with a carbine or shorter musket than the Foot, a bayonet, a hatchet and a straight sword. Owing to their kinship with infantry their senior NCOs ranked as sergeants, rather than as corporals of horse, and instead of the kettle-drums and trumpets of the Horse, they had the side-drums and hautbois of the Foot. Despite the multiplicity of their duties, the Dragoons' status ranked lower than the Horse, this being reflected in their different rates of pay: a colonel of Horse received 41 shillings a day compared with the 35 shillings of a dragoon colonel; a trooper received two shillings and sixpence a day plus fourteen shillings a week subsistence, against the dragoon's daily pay of one and sixpence and eight and twopence subsistence.

The British cavalry consisted entirely of Horse and Dragoons, but Austria was beginning to form the lightly equipped, irregular bands of Hungarian and Croat horsemen, raised on the eastern and southern frontiers for service against the Turks, into regular regiments of Hussars, an example also followed by France. An Austrian hussar regiment usually comprised about twelve companies. Mounted on small horses, armed with curved sabres, pistols and sometimes carbines, they were useful for outpost duties, hit-and-run raids, pursuits, in fact anything requiring rapidity of movement. When faced by a formed squadron of

Horse or Dragoons they would scatter, perhaps to re-form later but, if less well-disciplined, simply to flee.

Infantry

The infantry of most European armies contained one or more regiments of Royal Guards (although the Austrian Army was almost unique in not having such units) and a number of regiments of Foot, each of one or more battalions, recruited primarily from each country's own nationals but also from foreigners. The Dutch infantry, for example, had a Scots Brigade, and the French Huguenot regiments in the British service have already been mentioned. Furthermore a field army might also contain foreign corps, of all arms, hired out as mercenaries for the duration of a campaign. The Danish, Hessian and Hanoverian contingents served on this basis in Marlborough's army in the Low Countries.

In Britain the Sovereign's three regiments of Foot Guards were, unlike the Household Cavalry, as eligible for foreign service as any regiment of Foot, though they differed from the latter in having larger establishments, enjoying certain privileges and drawing higher rates of pay; the ordinary guardsman, for instance, received tenpence a day, as opposed to the eightpence of the line soldier. Senior among the British infantry of the standing army that had evolved since the Restoration of 1660 stood the 1st Guards, although the Coldstream could claim an unbroken lineage back to Britain's first standing army—Cromwell's

The Allied horse charging at Ramillies. A reconstruction by N. Dupray. (National Army Museum)

New Model. When William III ascended the English throne he brought with him his own Dutch, or Blue Guards, which took rank in England as the 3rd Foot Guards but returned to Holland after his death. Their title was subsequently assumed by the Scots Guards, who prior to 1707 had been on the Scottish establishment.

The respective seniority of the regiments of Foot was evolving, though not yet officially recognized, each regiment taking its name from its current colonel and proprietor, who might change quite frequently (see later table), and in some cases enjoying an additional title. For example the senior regiment, known in 1700 as Orkney's, was also designated the Royal Regiment (later Royal Scots), while at the same date Hamilton's was the Royal Regiment of Ireland (later 18th Foot, Royal Irish Regiment). In 1705 the latter became Ingoldsby's, a name hitherto borne by the regiment known after 1714 as the Royal Welch Fusiliers; such changes of colonels could well lead to confusion when formulating orders of battle so that, when a change-over occurred, a regiment might be known for a while as 'late So-and-So's' until its new title was familiar to all. The more senior the regiment, the less likely was it to be disbanded when Parliament issued its frequent demands for reductions.

Regiments of Guards and Foot each had a headquarters of a colonel—frequently, as in the cavalry, a general officer; a lieutenant-colonel, one or two majors, an adjutant, chaplain, a surgeon and his mate, a quartermaster and sometimes a drum-major. Each had a number of companies, which in the case of the 1st Guards and the Royal Regiment were sufficient to form two battalions, while the remainder had but one battalion. The standard number of companies was twelve plus a grenadier company, although the Coldstream and Scots Guards numbered more men overall in their battalions. The average company had a captain, a lieutenant and an ensign, two, sometimes three, sergeants, two corporals, a drummer sometimes accompanied by a hautbois player (the fife not then being used in the British Army) and about 60 men, or 'private sentinels' as they were called. Thus a single-battalion regiment at war establishment numbered just under 900 all ranks, though it was rare for them to be at full strength. In contrast, an Austrian regiment of Foot totalled some 2,500 men, made up of a 100-strong grenadier company and sixteen 150-strong companies divided into four battalions. The French, too, favoured regiments of several battalions, but the latter had a similar number of companies to the British.

In King William's war the battalion had had three types of infantryman—the pikeman, the musketeer and the grenadier—but the invention of the bayonet had made the pikeman superfluous. The first type of bayonet plugged into the muzzle of the musket, thus rendering it ineffective as a firearm, but at the beginning of the 18th century the socket type, which fitted over the muzzle, was coming into use so that the musketeer could fire with bayonet fixed. His firearm, too, had been improved, the flintlock replacing the matchlock; and, with powder and ball now pre-packaged into cartridges, the loading process was speeded up. Nevertheless it was a long, heavy weapon, five feet without bayonet, and with a rate of fire of only about two rounds a minute, with an effective range of around sixty yards, though a ball could carry 250 yards. In addition each musketeer carried a short sword, or hanger; in one of Laguerre's paintings infantrymen can be seen using these for close-quarter fighting in the woods

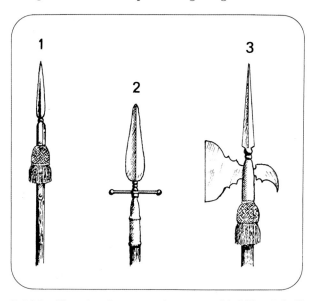

British officers' and sergeants' weapons: (1) Officer's half-pike; 9ft. long, the pike being 14ft. (2) Officer's spontoon; 7ft. long. (3) Sergeant's halbert; 7½ft. long. (Drawing by author)

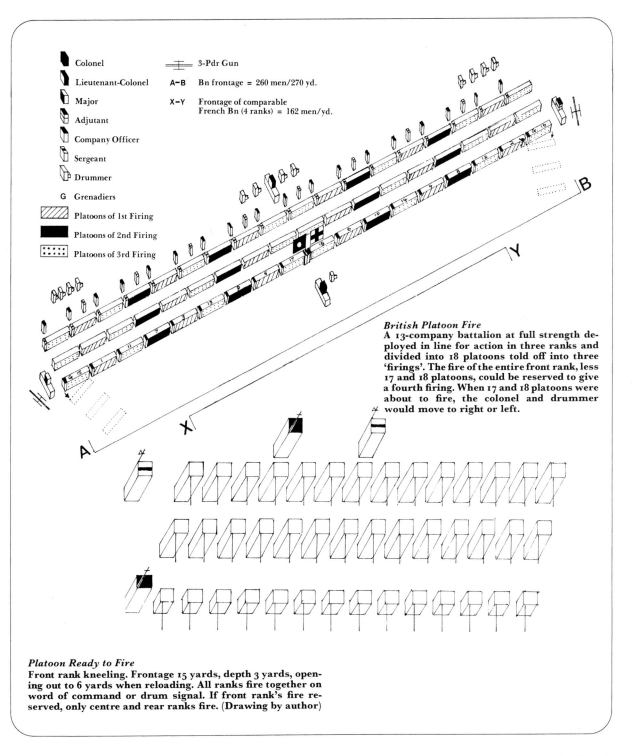

Key:

- Colonel
- Lieutenant-Colonel
- Major
- Adjutant
- Company Officer
- Sergeant
- Drummer
- G Grenadiers
- Platoons of 1st Firing
- Platoons of 2nd Firing
- Platoons of 3rd Firing

- 3-Pdr Gun
- A–B Bn frontage = 260 men/270 yd.
- X–Y Frontage of comparable French Bn (4 ranks) = 162 men/yd.

British Platoon Fire
A 13-company battalion at full strength deployed in line for action in three ranks and divided into 18 platoons told off into three 'firings'. The fire of the entire front rank, less 17 and 18 platoons, could be reserved to give a fourth firing. When 17 and 18 platoons were about to fire, the colonel and drummer would move to right or left.

Platoon Ready to Fire
Front rank kneeling. Frontage 15 yards, depth 3 yards, opening out to 6 yards when reloading. All ranks fire together on word of command or drum signal. If front rank's fire reserved, only centre and rear ranks fire. (Drawing by author)

at Malplaquet. Officers and sergeants all carried swords with, additionally, a pike, half-pike or spontoon (see line drawing) for the former (until spontoons were ordered for all by Marlborough in 1710), and a halbert for sergeants; grenadier officers carried a fusil, or short musket.

The grenadier company was composed of hand-picked, big, strong, 'valorous' men, armed with 'a good Sword, a Hatchet, a Firelock slung and a Pouch full of hand-Grenadoes' (usually three per man). The company either formed on the right of the battalion line or was split between the two wings, being expected to set an example of coolness and discipline to the rest of the battalion, and ever foremost in the storming of a breach or the last to hold a threatened position.

The task of the infantry in battle was to break the enemy's Foot with its fire, and therefore to bring the greatest number of its muskets to bear; a battalion advanced to the attack in line, each company beside the other, the men formed in three, four or five ranks. At maximum range periodic fire would be opened as the advance continued, until the real fire-fight began at about sixty yards, both sides blazing away until one broke. The French, Austrian and some of the German infantry favoured a four- or five-deep line, thus sacrificing some frontage, the whole of each rank firing a volley in turn, after which the entire battalion reloaded. In the Anglo-Dutch infantry a battalion was drawn up three ranks deep and its normal, day-to-day company organization broken down into eighteen platoons, which were told off into three 'firings' each of six platoons. The platoons forming a firing were staggered along the line so that fire could be kept up from every part of it. In each platoon the front rank would kneel, while the second and third stood, the latter firing between the intervals of the men in the second. Sometimes the front rank's fire would be reserved as a 'fourth firing' for unforeseen emergencies. After the first six platoons had fired, they would reload, while the second firing, followed by the third, continued the fusillade. Thus a continuous fire could be kept up and a third of the battalion was always ready to fire, as was the entire front rank if its fire had been reserved. Furthermore, the platoon system made for better fire control and the three-rank formation gave a wider frontage than a French battalion of equal strength, an advantage which could be increased by wheeling the grenadiers on the flanks slightly inwards. The total fire effect was further augmented by the British practice, also followed by the Dutch and Austrians, of siting two light guns firing canister on either flank. The platoon-fire system was also used to cover the retirement of a battalion, the six platoons of each firing covering the reloading and retreat of the other two, so that an advancing enemy was constantly checked by fire. (See accompanying line drawing.)

Officer of Austrian cuirassiers. Buff coat, red cuffs, silver buttons, black metal helmet and cuirass. Drawing by R. Ottenfeld. (Victoria and Albert Museum. Photo: R. J. Marrion)

Artillery and Engineers

In Marlborough's day there were as yet no Royal Regiment of Artillery or Royal Engineers, and all matters pertaining to gunnery, munitions, fortification and engineering were the province of the Board of Ordnance, quite separate from the rest of the Army. However, since Marlborough was both Master-General of the Ordnance and Captain-General of the Army, any difficulties between the two were greatly eased. To provide the necessary artillery and engineer support for a field army, the Board had to assemble special Trains. The first such Train sent to Holland in 1701 consisted of a staff; two artillery companies, each of three officers, six NCOs and 50 soldiers; a pioneer company of two sergeants and twenty pioneers; and a pontoon company of a bridge-master, two corporals and twenty pontoneers, together with 34 guns and howitzers. As the war progressed, so the Trains increased.

Cannons in use as field artillery ranged from the light 3pdrs. attached to battalions up to 24pdrs., while for siege warfare there were even heavier pieces of 48pdr. calibre; it was rare for the English Trains to contain anything heavier than a 16pdr. Such guns fired either round shot—a solid ball of stone or cast iron—or canister, which discharged a spray of small balls. The latter had little effect at ranges above 300 paces, while with round shot ranges varied from about 450 paces for the 3pdr. and 12pdr., up to 800 and 900 for the 16pdrs. and 24pdrs., although much greater ranges could be achieved by canting up the barrels to 45 degrees. However, as only direct fire was employed with cannon, about 600 paces was held to be the maximum effective range. As this was almost within the capability of a smaller calibre like the 6pdr., the usefulness of the bigger guns lay more in the weight of their missiles than in longer range.

Besides cannon there were two other types of artillery, used almost entirely for sieges: mortars,

of which a 13in. weapon might have a range of between 720–1,035 yards depending on the charge, and howitzers with a range of about 1,300 yards. Such weapons fired hollow shot filled with explosives.

All artillery pieces, except the 3pdrs., were extremely cumbersome, requiring at least eight or ten horses to draw them; these, with their drivers, had to be hired from civilian contractors. Their slow rate of movement, aggravated by the mass of wagons bearing their ammunition and associated stores, and their lack of mobility on the battlefield, all imposed limitations on the use of artillery in early 18th-century warfare. However, Marlborough fully appreciated the importance of his guns, closely supervising the siting of cannon to reinforce the line of battle, apportioning guns to batteries for the support or destruction of strong points, and co-ordinating their fire to best assist the tactical manoeuvres of Horse and Foot. In his four great victories of Blenheim, Ramillies, Oudenarde and Malplaquet, Marlborough employed an average of 98 guns of all calibres, a proportion of 1.34 guns to every 1,000 men of his total strength. In sieges the heavier guns, mortars and howitzers were grouped in batteries to weaken the defences, neutralize the enemy guns, harass the defenders and ultimately smash a breach through which the storming parties would pour.

As mentioned before, sieges were a major feature of the warfare of this period, which was also the age of the great engineers like the Frenchman Vauban, and the Dutchman Coehoorn. There is not space here to describe the elaborate system of fortifications nor the more or less standard procedures for the reduction of a fortress, but it can be found in great detail in David Chandler's *Art of War in the Age of Marlborough*, and the chief features of siege warfare are depicted in the accompanying diagrams.

Besides the many tasks involved in the defence or capture of fortresses, engineer officers had to advise on the construction of fortified camps, river crossings, road improvements, the siting of field defences and entrenchments and much else as well. The senior engineers were trained officers from the Board of Ordnance, but to command the detachments of miners, pioneers, and pontoneers, not to mention the large bodies of locally-impressed

Typical fortifications in diagrammatic form (not drawn to scale). *Top:* Bird's eye view. *Bottom:* Cross-section (excluding (D) and (F)).
(A) Interior of fortress. **(B)** Bastions sited along curtain wall with guns sweeping the glacis **(H)** about 12–15ft. above it. Wall 66ft. thick at base, tapering to 30ft. at gun platform **(C)** Temporary bridges (Sally-ports). **(D)** Demi-lune, to cover curtain wall between bastions. **(E)** Ditch, filled with water or stakes, about 95ft. wide and 20ft. deep. **(F)** Ravelin, covering vulnerable angle of bastion. **(G)** Covered way, firestep and parapet, about 20ft. wide. **(H)** Glacis, projecting 200–400 yards in front of parapet. (Drawing by author)

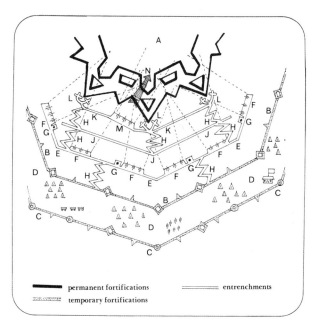

Stages of a siege. (A) represents part of the invested fortress.
Stage I (B) Lines of Contravallation, constructed all round
fortress outside artillery range, to prevent enemy egress.
(C) Lines of Circumvallation, all round fortress, to prevent
any relief force reaching the besieged. (D) Camp areas, headquarters, supply dumps and gun park of besiegers.
Stage II (E) First Parallel, dug at about 600 yards from defences (maximum cannon range). (F) Batteries for ricochet
and counter-battery fire. (G) Mortar batteries for harass-
ment of enemy troops and destruction of inner defences.
(H) Communication trenches.
Stage III (J) Second Parallel, at about 400 yards from defences.
Supply point for entrenching and siege equipment.
Stage IV (K) Third Parallel, on the enemy glacis (see Fortification diagram). (L) Traverses from which assaults on the
covered way would be made. (M) Breaching battery—moved
forward to enemy parapet once covered way cleared to batter
a breach in the bastion or curtain wall.
Stage V (N) Storming the breach if the enemy had not already
surrendered. (Drawing by author)

civilian labourers, officers had to be temporarily
seconded from other branches of the army.

Administration

In the vital fields of supply and transport, on
which the success or failure of a campaign so
greatly depended, everything was in the hands of
civilian contractors, working to the orders of
Marlborough's staff through the agency of Field
Commissaries appointed by the Commissioners of
Supply and Transport. The efficiency of their
arrangements depended on the ready availability
of cash, the honesty of the contractors and the re-
sources of the theatre of operations. In the relatively prosperous Low Countries, the Rhine
Valley and southern Germany, the system, under
Marlborough's ever-watchful eye, worked well

enough and, unlike some armies of the period
which almost starved at times, his soldiers seldom
lacked their daily bread. Their counterparts,
fighting in the barren lands of Spain and Portugal,
were less fortunate.

Additionally each regiment had its own civilian
sutlers, male and female, who provided luxuries
like meat, liquor and such other comforts as they
could acquire through lawful trading or simple
plundering. Among these was the famous Mother
Ross, otherwise known as Christian Davies, the
female dragoon, who, before she took up sutlering,
concealed her sex and enlisted to search for her
soldier husband, fighting with the Scots Greys
through the Schellenberg, Blenheim and Ramillies, where she was wounded. Her identity was
discovered in hospital, but she was reunited with
her husband and continued to follow the army as
a sutleress until the end of the war. She was cele-
brated as a skilful marauder for booty, a driver of a
hard bargain, but always ready to comfort or aid
a wounded or dying man. She died in 1739 and
was buried with military honours in Chelsea
Hospital.

Austrian hussar; see colour plate F2. Painting by R. Ottenfeld. (Victoria and Albert Museum. Photo: R. J. Marrion)

Although the treatment of battle casualties was inevitably limited by the medical knowledge of the age, Marlborough did all he could to ensure the sick and wounded were decently cared for. In addition to the 40-bed regimental hospitals manned by the regimental surgeons and their mates, there were also static and marching hospitals, where treatment was dispensed by civilian surgeons engaged for the duration of a campaign. During the march to the Danube in 1704 the sick were treated in a general hospital which followed the army by barge up the Rhine. First aid on the battlefield was administered at casualty clearing posts, from which the wounded were transported in requisitioned civilian wagons to the main army hospitals set up in neighbouring towns and villages. Even so, a casualty with a serious wound had but a one in three chance of surviving.

Grand Tactics

Marlborough's great abilities as strategist and diplomat are beyond the scope of this book and must be read elsewhere. His qualities as an inspiring leader and careful administrator have already been touched on briefly. Here something must be said of his tactics, and the typical Marlburian battle.

Top: **Cross-section showing how a breach was effected at the Siege of Landau in 1704. From the breaching battery (L), a sap (H) was constructed to the edge of the moat across which a causeway (B) was built, protected by flanking gabions (C), up to the breach (A), where fire was opened from behind sandbags (F) at the French embrasures (G).** *Bottom:* **(M) Method of covering the sap. (N) Fascine with sandbag attached. (O) Gabion. (P) Sandbags. (National Army Museum)**

Both in his set-piece battles like Blenheim and Ramillies and in an encounter battle like Oudenarde, the Duke's masterly appreciation of the ground and his ability to read the enemy commander's mind enabled him so to deploy his forces that he always retained the initiative, forcing the enemy to react to his moves. Having selected the most advantageous sector of the battlefield for his decisive thrust, he would maintain pressure at other points, thus inducing the enemy commander to weaken that part of his front, while at the same time building up a massive concentration of force for the ultimate breakthrough. For example at Blenheim, realizing the importance to the French of the two villages of Blenheim itself and Oberglau, which enfiladed the favourable open ground between them, he attacked both relentlessly, containing them and forcing Tallard to reinforce them by weakening his troops covering the open ground, through which Marlborough eventually drove in overwhelming strength. At Oudenarde his quick eye perceived that the inactivity of the French left required only a small force of cavalry to watch it,

17

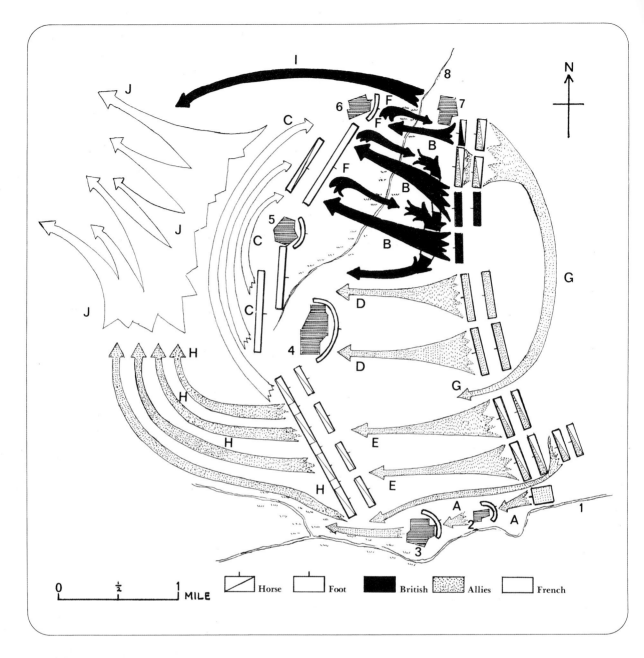

Battle of Ramillies
(1) River Mehaigne (2) Franquenay (3) Taviers (4) Ramillies (5) Offus (6) Autreglise (7) Foulz (8) River Little Geete.
(A) 2.30pm. Dutch Guards supported by 21 Danish squadrons storm French positions along the Mehaigne, thus securing left flank of Allied centre. (B) 2.30pm. British Horse (15 squadrons) and Foot (19 battalions) under Lord Orkney attack French left between Offus and Autreglise. (C) 2.45pm–3pm. French left reinforced from centre and right to meet (B) (as Marlborough had intended). (D) 3pm. Allied infantry in centre under Schultz advance on Ramillies, attacking village itself at about 3.30pm. Fighting continues until about 5pm. (E) 3pm. Overkirk attacks French right (68 squadrons) with 48 Dutch and 21 Danish squadrons. First charge repulsed and counter-attacked. Marlborough personally rallies Dutch, summons 39 Allied squadrons from right wing and orders Orkney to break off attack on right. Cavalry battle continues until about 5pm, when French give way. (F) 3.15pm approx. Orkney's withdrawal. First line remains east of the Geete to threaten French left; second line moves south under cover to reinforce Schultz at (D). (G) 3.15pm–3.30pm. 39 Allied squadrons moving from right wing to reinforce main cavalry attack. (H) 5pm. Allied cavalry break through and wheel right to form new line facing north. 6pm. Final cavalry attack begins while all infantry advance between Ramillies and Autreglise. French give way everywhere. (I) British Horse advance to cut off French retreat and begin pursuit. (J) 7pm. French in full retreat pursued by all Allied horse.

Comparative Strengths and Casualties
Allies

Strengths	62,000 (74 bns., 123 sqns., 120 guns)
Casualties	3,600
French	
Strengths	60,000 (70 bns., 132 sqns., 70 guns)
Casualties	18,000 (incl. 6,000 PWs, 54 guns)

(Drawing by author)

and that the nature of the ground permitted a concealed approach round the exposed French right. He therefore closely engaged the enemy centre and right while sending a large force of Dutch cavalry on a wide outflanking movement to fall upon the French rear.

Time and again his tactical vision enabled him to surprise and deceive the French marshals. This was seen at its best at the forcing of the supposedly impregnable Lines of 'Ne Plus Ultra', constructed by the French in the winter of 1710–11 to guard their northern frontier between the Channel coast and Namur. Having decided that the most advantageous point to cross the Lines was at Arleux, which was also conveniently close to his ultimate objective, the fortress of Bouchain, he tricked Marshal Villars into weakening his defences at that point by capturing a fortress which commanded the approaches, strengthening it, but then allowing it to be retaken; Villars obligingly destroyed it so that the Duke could not make use of it again, exactly as the latter had intended. Marlborough had by then concentrated his army further west opposite Arras, where, by dint of ostentatious reconnaissances and preparations for assault, he convinced Villars, and his own men,

the main blow would fall. However, during the night before the well-advertised attack, he secretly marched his entire force back eastwards, and by morning was crossing the denuded defences at Arleux as a hoodwinked Villars strove fruitlessly to catch him up.

Although the Duke favoured a massed force of cavalry for his final overthrow of an enemy battle-line, in the preceding stages of the action he placed great importance on mutual support between cavalry, infantry and artillery. At Blenheim he met a French cavalry counter-attack with a line of Horse backed by infantry flanked with guns. As the Allied squadrons were pressed back, they retired through the intervals between the battalions, which then broke the oncoming French horsemen with their volleys. To force the entrenchments protecting the French centre at Malplaquet, Marlborough pounded them with a 40-gun battery, followed by an immediate infantry assault with squadrons massed at the battalions' heels ready to exploit success.

To control the stages of a battle fought over a four- to six-mile frontage was a daunting task for any general when the fighting was always shrouded in dense clouds of gun-smoke, and the accurate

Marlborough watching his troops advancing to the Battle of Oudenarde. Note the drummer in the foreground. Detail from a painting by J. Wootton (Christie's)

and speedy transmission of orders depended on the power of the human voice, the drum, trumpet and the rate a man could cover ground on foot or horseback. Yet Marlborough's control of an action, aided by his specially selected aides-de-camp and relays of running footmen, was one of his most outstanding tactical qualities. Nowhere was this, and the other characteristic features of a Marlburian battle, demonstrated better than in his great triumph at Ramillies in 1706, as can be seen in the accompanying diagram and key, which illustrates the main stages of the battle. His weakening of the French centre by Orkney's attack on the right which, to ensure its desired effect, he did not even close to Orkney was only a feint; his securing the flanks of his chosen sector for the main attack by the assaults on Ramillies and Taviers, the latter achieved through mutual support between Dutch infantry and Danish horse; his concentration of force for the main blow by withdrawing troops from the right under cover; and his own personal powers of command in retrieving the initial failure of Overkirk's thrust, plus the not inconsiderable feat of wheeling over a hundred squadrons of triumphant horsemen through a 90-degree arc to form a new line so as to roll up the remaining French forces from the south —all are evidence of a master battlefield tactician at work.

Lastly, the trust and confidence he inspired in his men by giving them victory in battle and by his never-failing concern for their welfare was cemented by the knowledge shared by the whole army and expressed by the grenadier captain of the Royal Regiment of Ireland, Robert Parker, that in any enterprise the Duke 'would not push the thing unless he saw a strong probability of success'. Furthermore his army knew—as, claimed Parker, all France knew—that 'he was more than a match for all the generals of that nation. Upon all occasions he concerted matters with so much judgement and forecast, that he never fought a battle which he did not gain, nor laid siege to a town which he did not take.'

The British Army in the War of the Spanish Succession

The following table shows which British regiments were employed in Flanders and Spain in each year of the War of the Spanish Succession, together with such uniform details as are known. Regiments serving in the West Indies, America or at home are not included. Thus the British elements of Marlborough's army in Flanders or

A halt on the march. From the *Art of War*. (Victoria and Albert Museum)

that of Peterborough and Galway in Spain in any one year can be discovered by reading down the date column concerned.

Except for the Foot Guards, regiments are listed under their successive colonels' names, as was then the practice, but their later numerical designations are given in brackets; where no number appears, the regiment was disbanded after the war.

Regiments in CAPITAL LETTERS served under Marlborough in northern Europe throughout his chief campaigns of 1704–11; regiments in *italics* served partially under his command; the others served only in Spain.

In the uniform column the facing colour is given first, then any other known details. Unlike in later years when facing colours were prescribed by Royal Warrant and therefore remained constant, at this time they were chosen by the colonel and could thus vary when the regiment changed hands. Hence the details are in some cases uncertain and in others incomplete. The basic colour of all regiments' coats was crimson for Horse and the Royal Dragoons, red for other Dragoons and the Foot.

Abbreviations in the table: F = Flanders. B = Blenheim. R = Ramillies. O = Oudenarde. M = Malplaquet. S = Spain and Portugal. DG ... Dragoon Guards. D ... Dragoons. H ... Hussars. L ... Lancers. NR ... No Record.

Regiment	Date												Uniform
	1701	02	03	04	05	06	07	08	09	10	11	12	
Horse													
LUMLEY's (KDG)		F	F	FB	F	FR	F	FO	FM	F	F	F	Blue
Harvey's (2 DG)		S	S	S	S	S	S	S	S				Buff
WOOD's (3DG)		F	F	FB	F	FR	F	FO	FM	F	F	F	Green. Grey waistcoats
CADOGAN's (5DG)	—	F	F	FB	F	FR	F	FO	FM	F	F	F	1700 White, later green. Green waistcoats and breeches.
WYNDHAM's, PALMES's 06 (6DG)		F	F	FB	F	FR	F	FO	FM	F	F	F	Possibly sea-green
SCHOMBERG's (7DG)		F	F	FB	F	FR	F	FO	FM	F	F	F	NR
Dragoons													
Royal Regt., Raby's (1D)		F	FS	S	S	S	S	S	S	S			Blue. Gold lace
ROYAL SCOTS, HAY's, STAIR's 06 (2D)		F	F	FB	F	FR	F	FO	FM	F	F	F	Blue
Lloyd's, Carpenter's 03 (3D/H)		S				S	S						Possibly blue
Essex's (4D/H)						S	S						Possibly light green
ROYAL IRISH ROSS's (5D/L)		F	F	FB	F	FR	F	FO	FM	F	F	F	NR
Kerr's (7D/H)											F	F	Possibly white

Regiment	1701	02	03	04	05	06	07	08	09	10	11	12	Uniform
Conyngham's, Killigrew's 06, Pepper's 07 (8D/H)			S	S	S	S	S	S	S	S			Yellow
Pearce's (from Barrymore's Foot)						S	S	S					Yellow
Peterborough's, Nassau's 07, J. Stanhope's 10						S	S	S	S	S			NR
Guiscard's (Huguenots)						S	S	S	S	S			NR
Rochford's, Lepell's 10									S	S	S	S	NR
Foot Guards													
1ST GUARDS: 1ST BN.	F	F	F	FB	F	FR	F	FO	FM	F	F	F	Blue. Yellow lace. Blue breeches.
Detachment		S		S	S	S	S						
Coldstream Guards: 1st Bn.								FO	FM	F	F	F	Blue. Yellow lace. Blue breeches.
Detachment		S		S	S	S	S						
Scots Guards									S	S			White, 1707 blue
Foot													
ROYAL REGT. ORKNEY'S Two Bns. (1st)	F	F	F	FB	F	FR	F	FO	FM	F	F	F	Blue
Queen Dowager's Bellasis's, *Portmore's* 03 Kirke's 10 (2nd)		S	FS	S	S	S	S						Sea-green
BUFFS, C. CHURCHILL'S, ARGYLL'S 07 SELWYN'S 11 (3rd)		S		FB	F	FR	F	FO	FM	F	F	F	Buff
Seymour's Marines (4th)		S		S	S	S	S						Possibly yellow
Pearce's (5th)							S	S	S	S	S	S	Green
Rivers's, Southwell's 06, Harrison's 08 (6th)		S		S	S	S			S				Yellow
Royal Fusiliers, Tyrawley's (7th)		S				S	S	S	S	S			Blue
QUEEN'S, WEBB'S (8th)	F	F	F	FB	F	FR	F	FO	FM	F	F	F	Yellow

Steuart's (9th)	F	F	F	S	S	S	S	S					Possibly orange
NORTH & GREY'S (10th)	F	F	F	FB	F	FR	F	FO	FM	F	F	F	Possibly yellow
Stanhope's, Hill's 05 (11th)	F	F	S	S	S	S	S		F	F	F	F	Yellow. Yellow lace, (Sgts gold), breeches and waistcoat
Livesay's (12th)								F			S	S	White. Possibly blue breeches
Barrymore's, Into Pearce's Dragoons 06. New Barrymore's 08 (13th)	F	F	S	S	S	S	S		S	S	S		Yellow. White breeches
HOWE'S, SOMERSET'S 09 (15th)	F	F	F	FB	F	FR	F	FO	FM	F	F	F	Red or yellow. Officers red
DERBY'S, GODFREY'S 05 (16th)	F	F	F	FB	F	FR	F	FO	FM	F	F	F	White. White breeches

'Ambuscade' from the *Art of War*. Note the grenadier caps worn by some of the infantry in the wood. The weapons and equipment in the surround are also worth study. (Victoria and Albert Museum)

Regiment	Date												Uniform
	1701	02	03	04	05	06	07	08	09	10	11	12	
Bridge's, Blood's 03, Wightman's 07 (17th)	F	F	S	S	S	S	S	S	S	S			Possibly grey
ROYAL IRISH, HAMILTON'S, INGOLDSBY'S 05 (18th)	F	F	F	FB	F	FR	F	FO	FM	F	F	F	Blue
Erle's (19th)		S							FM	F	F	F	Yellow. Yellow breeches
G. Hamilton's, Newton's 06 (20th)		S					S	S	S	S	S	S	1706 White. Pewter buttons. Officers: Scarlet. Gold lace senior officers, silver junior. Grey stockings
SCOTS FUSILIERS, ROW'S, MORDAUNT'S 04 and 09–10, DE LALO'S 06, ORRERY'S 10 (21st)			F	FB	F	FR	F	FO	FM	F	F	F	Red. Grey breeches. Yellow stockings
INGOLDSBY'S, SABINE'S 05 (23rd)	F	F	F	FB	F	FR	F	FO	FM	F	F	F	NR
SEYMOUR'S, MARLBOROUGH'S 02, TATTON'S 04, PRIMROSE'S 08 (24th)	F	F	F	FB	F	FR	F	FO	FM	F	F	F	NR
CAMERONIANS, FERGUSON'S, BORTHWICK'S 05, STAIR'S 06, PRESTON'S 06 (26th)			F	FB	F	FR	F	FO	FM	F	F	F	White
Inniskillings, Whetham's (27th)									S	S	S		NR
Gibson's, *De Lalo's* 04, Mordaunt's 06, Windsor's 09 (28th)					F	F	FR	S	S	S	S		NR
Farrington's (29th)					F	F	FR	S	F	F		S	S	Yellow. Blue breeches. White stockings
Saunderson's Marines, Pownall's 04, Wills's 05 (30th)				S	S	S	S						Yellow

1. England: The Duke of Marlborough
2. Austria: Prince Eugene of Savoy
3. England: Marlborough's Trumpeter

A

1. England: Sergeant, Scots Regiment of Fusiliers, 1706
2. Holland: Ensign, Regiment of Foot, 1704
3. Denmark: Musketeer, Regiment of Foot, 1703

B

1. England: Grenadier, 1st Foot Guards, 1704
2. Austria: Grenadier officer, Walloon Regiment
   of Foot, 1708
3. Holland: Musketeer, Foot Guards, 1706

C

1. England: Officer, Regiment of Horse, 1705
2. Austria: Trooper, Regiment of Cuirassiers, 1705
3. England: Drummer, Regiment of Foot, 1704

D

1. Prussia: Grenadier, Regiment of Foot, 1709
2. England: Ensign, Regiment of Foot, 1708
3. Hanover: Trooper, Regiment of Dragoons, 1708

1. Prussia: Fifer, Foot Guards, 1704
2. Austria: Trooper, Regiment of Hussars, 1709
3. England: Sentinel, Regiment of Foot, 1709

F

1. Holland: Officer of Artillery, 1705
2. England: Trooper, Regiment of Horse, 1709
3. England: Gunner, Train of Artillery, 1709

G

1. Prussia: Officer, Foot Guards, 1702
2. England: Corporal, Regiment of Dragoons, 1704
3. Holland: Trooper, Regiment of Cuirassiers, 1708

Regiment	Date												Uniform
	1701	02	03	04	05	06	07	08	09	10	11	12	
Villiers's Marines, Luttrell's 03, Churchill's 06, Goring's 11 (31st)		S	S	S	S	S	S	S					Yellow
Fox's Marines, Borr's 04 (32nd)		S	S	S	S	S	S	S	S	S			Green. Pewter buttons. White lace (Sgts. silver)
Huntingdon's, Leigh's 03, Duncanson's 05, Wade's 05 (33rd)		F	F	S	S	S	S	S	S	S			Yellow. Yellow breeches. White stockings
Lucas's *H. Hamilton's* (34th)					S	S	S	F	F	F	F	F	Light grey. Grey breeches & waist-coat
Donegal's Gorges's 06 (35th)				S	S	S	S						Orange
Charlemont's, Alnutt's 06, Argyll's 09, Disney's 10 (36th)		S			S	S	S						Green
MEREDITH'S, WINDRESS'S 10 (37th)			F	FB	F	FR	F	FO	FM	F	F	F	Possibly yellow
Coote's, Sankey's 03 (39th)							S	S	S	S	S	S	NR
Stringer's, Argyll's 06, Orrery's 07 Sibourg's 10				F	F	FR	F	FO	FM	F	F	F	NR
Temple's, Newton's 10				F	F	F	F	FO	FM	F	F	F	NR
Evans's				F	F	FR	F	FO	FM	F	F	F	NR
Macartney's, Sutton's 09				F	F	FR	S	F	F	F	F	F	NR
Prendergast's, Macartney's 09 Kane's 11								FO	FM	F			Green. Scarlet breeches. Sgts. silver lace
Wynne's								F	F	F	F		Yellow. Blue and white lace. Yellow waistcoat. Blue breeches. Wolf's head on grenadier caps
Townshend's, Honeywood's 09								F	F	F	F	F	NR

Regiment	1701	02	03	04	05	06	07	08	09	10	11	12	Uniform
Brudenell's, *Johnson's* 08, C. Churchill's 09			S	S	S	S		F					NR
Mountjoy's			S	S	S	S	S						NR
Gorges's, Allen's 06, *Moore's* 07 Molesworth's 10					S	S		F			S	S	NR
J. Caulfield's, Bowles's 05					S	S	S		S	S			NR
Elliot's					S	S	S	S	S	S	S		NR
Mohun's, *Dormer's* 08						S		F	F	S			NR
T. Caulfield's, *Creighton's* 08						S		F					NR
Breton's, Butler's 11						S	S	S	S	S	S	S	Willow green breeches
Stanwix's							S	S	S	S	S		Yellow. Brass buttons
Dungannon's, Montandre's 06						S	S			S			NR
Watkin's, Rich's 09						S	S	S	S	S	S	S	NR
Hotham's						S	S	S	S		S		NR
Mark Kerr's						S	S				S	S	NR
Paston's, Franks's 10							S	S	S	S	S		NR
Inchiquin's, Stanhope's 10, Nassau's 11									S	S	S	S	Officers, scarlet
Lepell's, Richards's 10, Stanhope's 11									S	S	S	S	NR
Munden's									S	S			NR
Gore's									S	S			NR
Rooke's											S	S	NR
Price's											S	S	NR
Fielding's											S		NR
E. Jones's											S	S	NR

Slane's	S	S	NR
Tyrell's	S	S	NR

Comparison of total regiments deployed in Flanders and Spain between 1701–12:

Type	1701		1702		1703		1704		1705		1706		1707		1708		1709		1710		1711		1712	
	F	S	F	S	F	S	F	S	F	S	F	S	F	S	F	S	F	S	F	S	F	S	F	S
Horse	–	–	5	–	5	1	5	1	5	1	5	1	5	1	5	1	5	1	5	1	5	–	5	–
Dragoons	–	–	3	1	3	1	2	2	2	2	2	7	2	7	2	5	2	5	2	5	3	1	3	–
Guards	1	–	1	1	1	–	1	1	1	1	1	1	1	1	2	–	2	1	2	1	2	–	2	–
Foot	12	–	13	10	14	8	18	13	18	19	18	27	15	29	26	17	24	21	22	22	21	23	20	17

George Hamilton, First Earl of Orkney. Colonel of the Royal Regiment from 1692–1737 and one of Marlborough's senior commanders. He wears the Star of the Order of the Thistle. Although full armour was no longer worn, it was the convention of portrait painters to depict general officers wearing it. (National Army Museum)

Uniform and Equipment

Although some individual regiments in the armies of the Thirty Years War and the English Civil War had been dressed uniformly, the concept of a uniform dress for all soldiers of a national army had only grown up in the second half of the 17th century; by the War of the Spanish Succession it was commonplace in all European nations. It was to prove an important factor in the establishment of discipline and the growth of *esprit de corps*. However, since—unlike later periods—the cut and style of a soldier's clothing, which followed current civilian fashions, was broadly similar in all armies, and since the colours chosen were common to many, the motivation behind the concept of uniformity was not to distinguish friend from foe but simple economy. Whether troops were supplied with clothing by the state, as in Austria after 1703, or through the regimental colonels as in Britain, it was obviously cheaper to purchase material of a uniform colour and quality.

The cheapest material for soldiers' coats, as far as colour was concerned, was undyed woollen cloth; hence the prevalence of varying shades of white to grey among the infantry, the bulk and least expensive element of any army, and even among some of the cavalry of France, Austria, Holland, Denmark, Spain and many of the smaller states of the Empire. Sweden and Prussia adopted dark blue in the 1690s, Bavaria sky-blue, and Russia alone had green, though this colour was also to be found in some units of the Austrian

English grenadiers and Dutch guardsmen fighting at close quarters with the French in the woods at Malplaquet. Note the chained logs the French used as defences. Detail of the painting by Laguerre. (Marquess of Anglesey)

Army. Red, a cheap dye, had been an increasingly popular, though by no means universal, colour for clothing English troops since the 15th century, and after its general adoption by the New Model Army in 1645 had continued at the Restoration as the uniform colour for the English and Scottish armies. Under William III a few regiments had worn grey or dark blue as worn by his Dutch troops, but under Anne all were in red. The same colour was favoured by Hanover and Saxony and in certain Danish regiments.

It did not follow that the adoption of a national colour for the bulk of an army meant that all its elements were clothed alike. In many late 17th century armies, including the British, officers were often distinguished from their men by coats of a different colour, a variation particularly applicable to general and staff officers. By the time of Marlborough's campaigns greater, if not total uniformity within regiments prevailed, although as late as 1710 the Duke had to remind regimental officers that they should 'be all clothed in red, plain and uniform'. In the detail and embellishment of their clothing British officers were still allowed considerable latitude, unlike their Austrian counterparts whose dress was extremely plain. Further variations from the national colour occurred in the different branches of some armies, particularly in the case of Guards regiments, whose uniform colours followed their monarch's livery, the more expensive cavalry, and in the artillery, where the handling of guns and associated equipment demanded a clothing colour which least showed the dirt. However, in the British service varying shades of red were worn in all branches.

Typical clothing of the late 17th/early 18th century soldier of all arms began with a knee-length, full-skirted coat, with pleats at the sides falling from buttons at hip level, and vents within the pleats either side and another at the back. The coats buttoned down the front and had long, full cuffs turned back and fastened with buttons to show the coat lining, which was frequently of a contrasting colour, thus distinguishing one regiment from another—the origin of regimental facings. Two large pockets were set low on the front of the skirts. Under the coat went a thigh-length waistcoat, usually with long sleeves and either of the same colour as the coat or of its lining —a garment which, in the British army at least, was cut down from the previous year's coat. The top buttons of coat and waistcoat were normally unfastened to reveal a white linen shirt, while the throat was closed by a simple, knotted neckcloth, sometimes of black, blue or red in foreign armies, but usually white, which for British troops was made of an inferior cloth known as sleazy; officers of course indulged in superior neckwear of lace or fine linen. Officers of most armies embellished their coats and waistcoats with gold or silver lace or embroidery on the seams, button-holes, cuffs, pocket flaps and edges, a fashion adopted to a less lavish extent for NCOs, whose clothing was generally of better-quality cloth than the men's. The practice of lacing the coat became a regular dress feature for all ranks of the British army later in the 18th century, the privates' lace being of a distinctive pattern for each regiment. But in the period under review, as far as the men were concerned, it seems to have been largely confined to the grenadier companies and drummers, the lace itself being of plain white or yellow worsted. In the absence of general regulations such matters, like so much other detail of soldiers' dress, lay within the province and purse of the regimental colonel.

The soldier's legs were clad in breeches, which tied or buttoned below the knee; stockings of wool or worsted, the tops of which were sometimes pulled up over the breeches and held up with a garter below the knee; and shoes with high tongues, usually fastened with buckles. Again, the quality of such items varied between the ranks, while the colour might match the coats, the linings or be different altogether. The practice of wearing long gaiters, or 'spatterdashes', to protect the lower leg and prevent shoes being sucked off in the mud, became popular as the war progressed. Mounted men wore long, blackened boots, which

for the Horse were stiffened to become the 'jacked' boot with wide, rigid tops which prevented the knees being crushed in the close order of the charge, but for Dragoons, in view of their dismounted rôle, were of more supple leather.

The universal headdress for all ranks of all armies was the broad-brimmed black felt hat which, by the early 18th century, was increasingly being worn with the brim turned up on three sides, fastened on at least one side by a button or loop, and often bound with gold, silver or worsted lace according to the rank of the wearer. Officers' hats were beginning to assume the neat 'tricorne' shape, but the soldiers', certainly after a few weeks' campaigning, lacked the more regular shape which their hats had acquired by the 1740s. The only exceptions to the hat were the 17th-century iron helmets still worn by Austrian and Bavarian heavy cavalry, and the caps of varying designs worn by grenadiers of Dragoons and Foot. Since the grenadier needed to sling his musket across his back when igniting and throwing his grenade (which he did underarm), a broad-brimmed hat would be inconvenient. The original grenadier

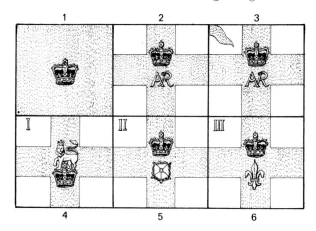

The regiments of Foot Guards carried more Colours than the Line. Above are the Colonel's (1), Lieutenant-Colonel's (2), Major's (3), and the first to third Captains' (4–6) Colours of the 1st Guards prior to 1707.

Senior to these was the Queen's Company Colour, the Royal Standard, which was crimson like the Colonel's but slightly larger and with the Royal Cypher, interlaced *and* reversed, beneath the Crown; after 1704 it had the arms of England, Scotland, Ireland and France in each corner. The remaining twenty Captains' Colour badges and the Coldstream Colours can be found in Lawson, *History of Uniforms of the British Army*, Vol. I. The Colours above measured 6ft. 11in. flying and 6ft. 5in. in the hoist. Shaded part crimson, insignia gold. The cords and tassels of the Standard were gold, the Colonel's gold and crimson, and the remainder crimson. After 1707 the St Andrew's Cross was added to those Colours bearing the St George's Cross. (Drawing by author) headdress was simply a stocking or bag cap, often bound with fur, but by the early 18th century these had generally been smartened up to give a more ornate and imposing aspect with an upright front of stiffened and embroidered cloth, as in the British, Danish and Prussian service, or of fur, as in the Austrian, or of brass, as in the Dutch infantry.

Turning to equipment, the officer required no more than the means to suspend his sword for which, by the early 18th century, the previously popular baldrick, often richly embroidered, was giving way to a waistbelt with a frog, usually worn under the coat or even the waistcoat; when the coat buttons were fastened, the hilt emerged through the side vents in the skirts. Under this heading may also be added the sash, a distinctive feature of officers' dress in most armies, and, in the

infantry, the gorget, which had evolved from a piece of armour guarding the throat into a semi-circular metal ornament suspended by ribbons round the neck, and which served as the chief distinguishing mark of an officer's rank when on duty.

The ordinary soldier's accoutrements were generally of buff leather and consisted firstly of a belt with a frog for his sword, which was worn round the waist, either over or under his coat, or, in the case of some regiments of Horse, over the right shoulder. The introduction of the bayonet required the addition of a further frog to carry that weapon on the belts of the Foot and Dragoons. With the advent of the made-up cartridge, the 17th-century bandoliers with their twelve dangling, metal or leather powder-charges, bullet bag and priming flask were being replaced by an ammunition pouch or 'cartouch box' suspended from a belt over the left shoulder. These usually contained 24 rounds, but since grenadiers each carried three grenades their pouches were larger, unless they had a separate pouch for their cartridges as the Dutch did. The sword belt and pouch formed the basic accoutrements of the infantryman and the dragoon. The trooper of Horse, in addition to his sword-belt, also wore a carbine-belt over the left shoulder, fitted with a swivel for attachment to the sliding ring on the carbine and a small ammunition pouch. The wearing of armour by the Horse has been discussed earlier under Organization and Armament.

In addition to his basic equipment, the infantryman on campaign would have a knapsack to carry his belongings, slung over one shoulder and made of canvas or hide. Furthermore there were items of camp equipment to be shared out among the men of a company, which in the British infantry included tent-poles, camp kettles, picks, shovels and an item mentioned in a contemporary list of stores as 'tin flasks'; these may have been the rectangular water-bottles that are shown in the Morier paintings of grenadiers, c.1751, but no other pictorial evidence of these items being carried is known. In all the infantryman carried some 50lb. weight, including his musket.

Some idea of the equipment required by a cavalryman can be gained from a list of kit for private soldiers of Killigrew's Dragoons in 1707

Grenadier cap of the Royal Regiment of Ireland, believed to have belonged to Captain Robert Parker. (National Army Museum)

The Battle of Malplaquet. The dark-uniformed figure moving the log may be a grenadier of the Dutch Foot Guards. Two English grenadiers are behind him and more can be seen at left. After Laguerre. (Courtauld Institute of Art)

(previously mentioned articles of personal equipment have been omitted): 'Cloaks; holster with straps; housings [the embroidered horse cloth under the rear part of the saddle] and holster caps [cloth covers]; buckets [for muskets] and straps; horse furniture as headstall, reins, breast plates and cruppers, bits, bosses, collars and cloak straps; saddles with skirts and furniture with straps, with girths, stirrup-leathers and irons.' The furniture mentioned in connection with the saddle probably refers to the soldier's valise, the equivalent of the infantryman's knapsack. In addition there were such items as forage bags, water buckets, picketing ropes and pegs, and articles of camp equipment and tools to be shared among the troop.

Most of the points mentioned in this section are illustrated in the colour plates, the notes for which follow. However, mention must be made of the sources from which these have been reconstructed. For the British Army of this period there is a certain amount of documentary evidence, most of which has been published in the *Journal of the Society for Historical Research*. Of contemporary pictorial evidence there is very little, and nothing comparable with the detailed material available for the reign of George II and subsequently. The Marlborough tapestries at Blen-

heim Palace and other tapestries of the period, such as those in the Victoria and Albert Museum, while giving an admirable 'feel' of military operations at this time, together with good, detailed representations of the Duke and senior officers, do little more than give a general impression of soldiers of the period, who may, with one or two exceptions, be of any one of the national contingents forming the Duke's army. The similarity of uniform cut and colour between different armies makes it impossible to determine with any certainty the nationality of the troops in these tapestries. Furthermore it must be remembered that they were woven in the Low Countries, where the artists concerned with their manufacture would tend to reproduce the native soldiery they saw around them. In the other chief pictorial source, the paintings of Louis Laguerre in Marlborough House, some figures are obviously meant to represent British troops (although a red coat does not necessarily make a figure British), but there are indications that the artist based his figures on soldiers of a slightly later period, about 1716–20. Thus any reconstruction of British uniforms must contain a considerable speculative element as to detail, while drawing upon the sources mentioned above and the work of other artists such as Wootton, Ross, Eyck and Marcellus Laroon, in conjunction with evidence of the uniforms of the two preceding reigns and to some extent those of the later, better-documented period, whose dress was a logical development from the Marlburian period. For representatives of the Allied contingents of Marlborough's army, reliance has largely had to be placed on such authorities as Ottenfeld and Knötel and contemporary work by the Dutch painters Huchtenberg and De Hooghe, supplemented by information kindly provided by the foreign sources mentioned in the Acknowledgements.

The Plates

A1: England: The Duke of Marlborough
The Duke's costume is based on those depicted in the tapestries at Blenheim Palace. Since it is known that he took a keen interest in their manufacture, it is likely that he would have insisted on the correct portrayal of his own dress. The amount of gold lace on the scarlet coat varies, e.g. in the Donauworth tapestry there is only one gold band on the cuffs, whereas in that showing Blenheim there are two. The amount of gold lace was a matter of personal choice, not an indication of rank; the latter is shown by his baton. In all the tapestries he is wearing buttoned gaiters, similar to those of French dragoons, in preference to the long boots normally worn by mounted men. He wears the blue sash of the Order of the Garter across his waistcoat and a crimson silk sash around the waist under the coat. The waist sash also varies in richness in different tapestries. His sword and horse furniture are taken from the actual surviving items.

A2: Austria: Prince Eugene of Savoy
This representation of Marlborough's great confederate is based on a portrait by J. van Schuppen. The original shows the cuirass and lobster-tailed helmet still being worn by the Austrian cuirassiers (see D2), but here a gold-laced hat has been substituted, as Eugene appears so dressed in the Laguerre painting of Blenheim and the Oudenarde tapestry.

The cuirass has been retained, as these were frequently worn by general officers at this period. His gold-embroidered brown coat is curious in that it lacks the deep cuffs common to most coats at this time. Around his neck is the Hapsburg Order of the Golden Fleece.

A3: England: Marlborough's Trumpeter
Generals in command of armies had State trumpeters attached to their personal staffs, Marlborough having two. They were dressed similarly to the trumpeters of the Life Guards, in the Royal Livery of gold-laced crimson coats, faced with blue velvet, much the same as the State dress worn today by the Band and Trumpeters of the Household Cavalry. Queen Anne's cypher was worn on the front and back of the coats, and a feature of the latter was the hanging false sleeves at the back, which were simply bands of laced cloth falling from the shoulders and attached to the waist. The trumpet banner was emblazoned with the Royal Arms (which at that date still included the fleur-de-lys of France) and the Queen's motto, 'Semper Eadem'. At the battle of Elixem in 1705 Marlborough's trumpeter took prisoner a giant Bavarian cuirassier who had attacked the Duke.

B1: England: Sergeant, Scots Regiment of Fusiliers, 1706
On the pre-1707 Scottish establishment was a regiment of 'Fuzileers', raised in 1678 by the Earl of Mar and ordered to be trained as grenadiers. Its coats were faced with red, and from the colour of its breeches it was known colloquially as 'The Earl of Mar's Grey Breeks'. The uniform shown here is based on a contemporary manikin figure in the Scottish United Services Museum. On the latter the bag of the cap is upright, but, since it stands above the front piece, it was probably not fastened to it, as was the later practice. It is noteworthy that the front does not match the facings, as was usually the case with such caps, and its colour, like the thistle, reflects the regiment's nationality. In some regiments sergeants had silver lace on their coats, but the chief distinguishing mark of their rank was the halbert (although the manikin in the S.U.S.M. has a simple pike). This regiment served throughout Marlborough's

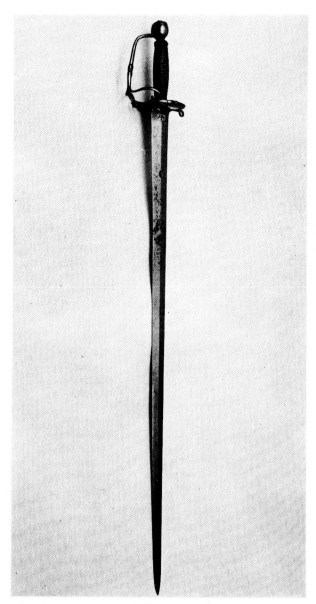

Cavalry sword, c.1700. (H.M. Tower of London)

campaigns and from 1712 it received blue facings and was styled 'Royal North British (later Scots) Fuzileers'.

B2: Holland: Ensign, Regiment of Foot, 1704
With the exception of the blue-coated Foot Guards (see C3) and the red-coated Scots regiments in Dutch service, the infantry of the United Provinces wore grey coats which varied in shade between ash-grey and the 'pearl' colour common to other European armies. The facings were mainly red or blue. Because of the popularity of this colour, field signs were worn in the headdress to distin-

guish friend from foe: in this case a sprig of leaves. The ensign's officer status is marked by his orange sash and his gilt gorget. The links between England and Holland established through William III are perpetuated on the Colour by the Garter in the centre and his cypher, 'W.R.' The rank and file of the Dutch infantry were dressed similarly though more plainly, with their accoutrements worn over the coat. Their grenadiers wore a blue cap with folding sides and brass front, as can be seen at the officer's feet in the illustration.

B3: Denmark: Musketeer, Regiment of Foot, 1703
The Danish national infantry also wore grey with different coloured facings for each regiment. An unusual feature of their coats was the double row of buttons down the front with a lace loop in between, thus making the coats double-breasted. The metal powder flask, an item common to much infantry equipment of this period, was attached by leather thongs or cords to the pouch-belt. The Danish Life Guards of Foot, a battalion of which fought under Marlborough, had single-breasted yellow coats, faced and laced with red, with red breeches and stockings. The lace either side of the coat fastening was arranged in a ladder pattern.

C1: England: Grenadier, 1st Foot Guards, 1704
This figure is an amalgam of those in Laguerre's well-known painting of Blenheim, commonly held to be the 1st Guards, and a prominent grenadier in the Blenheim tapestry, which, in view of the Garter Star on his cap and the fact that Marlborough was himself Colonel of the 1st Guards, probably represents that regiment. The coat in the tapestry, however, has turned-back lapels, which seem unlikely for British uniforms of this period, although some German regiments had them. Such lapels also appear on a sergeant in the Wynendael tapestry, often described as being of the Royal Scots, though his white facings and moustache obviously preclude this. This guardsman is therefore shown with the roll collar, itself unusual for the period, from the Laguerre painting. The grenadier cap has its bag sewn to the upright front, a fashion increasingly common but not yet universal. The rounded ends of the lace loops in the tapestry figure are also evident

in the next known representation of the 1st Guards —the paintings made in 1735 by Lens to illustrate the *Granadiers Exercise*—although by then they have changed to white. The yellow lace, blue waistcoat and breeches are mentioned in descriptions of deserters from the Coldstream Guards, whose dress followed that of the 1st Guards. The Laguerre painting has the guardsmen in stockings pulled up over the knees, but the grenadier in the tapestry has marching gaiters as shown here. Since Marlborough himself favoured these leg coverings, it seems likely he would have had his own regiment equipped with them. In 1710 he ordered all regiments of Foot to have them in white, but the Flanders mud had probably induced regiments to adopt them before then. A tent-pole with tent-pegs tied to it was commonly lashed to the knapsack, but, when a regiment advanced into action, a commanding officer would order 'the soldiers to lay down their knap-

Austrian artillery. Pearl grey uniform with red cuffs, brass buttons; yellow lace on hat; buff belts; red flask cord with black leather flask. Painting by R. Ottenfeld. (Victoria and Albert Museum. Photo: R. J. Marrion)

sacks, tent-poles and what is cumbersome'. A slightly later military treatise deplored some soldiers' habit of tying tent-poles to their muskets, which obviously left them unready for immediate action. The battalion companies of Foot Guards wore the ordinary hat but bound with yellow lace. Since there is no mention of lace loops in a description of a Coldstream coat in 1712, these may have been solely a distinction of the grenadier company.

C2: Austria: Grenadier officer, Walloon Regiment of Foot, 1708
Although the Austrian infantry as a whole were dressed in pearl grey (see monotone illustrations), the seven infantry regiments raised from the Walloons of the Spanish Netherlands by the Archduke Charles of Austria after Ramillies were uniformed in green, faced with crimson. These regiments all fought at Oudenarde and Malplaquet. Grenadier officers in the Austrian service wore the hat instead of the fur caps of the men, but carried a fusil rather than the partisan of the battalion company officers; a cartouch box was worn round the waist above the usual Austrian officer's sash in the Hapsburg colours of black and gold.

C3: Holland: Musketeer, Foot Guards, 1706
The blue and orange livery of the House of Orange was reserved in the Dutch infantry for the Foot Guards, which had three battalions. They fought all through Marlborough's campaigns, suffering particularly heavy losses in the attack on the French right flank at Malplaquet. Their grenadiers may have had caps like those mentioned in B2, although in one of Laguerre's paintings a figure possibly representing a Dutch Guards grenadier has a fur cap (see monotone illustrations). Note the long sleeves of the orange waistcoat which emerge below the coat cuffs.

D1: England: Officer, Regiment of Horse, 1705
As mentioned under A1, the quantity and arrangement of the gold or silver lace on English officers' coats at this period were largely determined by their personal taste and wealth. Under field conditions an officer might wear a less expensive garment. Furthermore it was unusual for officers

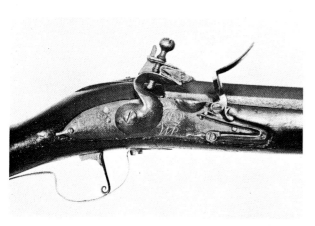

Lock of a flintlock musket; note the cypher of William III. (Mr Peter Dinely)

to have their cuffs and coat linings conforming with the facings on their men's coats, and although this officer's buff waistcoat and breeches might have been worn to match the buff facings of Harvey's Horse, they could equally have been chosen by an officer of the blue-faced Lumley's or green-faced Wood's or Cadogan's purely for their practicality. His sword is suspended from a waistbelt worn under the waistcoat.

D2: Austria: Trooper, Regiment of Cuirassiers, 1705
In the early years of the war the appearance of the Austrian cuirassiers still retained echoes of the Thirty Years War with their thick buff leather coats, back-and-breast cuirasses and iron helmets. The latter were giving way to the felt hat with iron skull-cap within, although the precise date of change is uncertain; Ottenfeld shows the helmet still being worn in 1705. Cuirassiers were the heaviest of Horse and in addition to their long, straight swords suspended from a waistbelt worn under the cuirass, they had a pair of pistols in holsters on the front of the saddle, and a carbine, either attached to a swivel on the broad shoulder-belt, or strapped to the saddle with the butt resting in a bucket in front of the off-side stirrup. A cuirassier officer can be found in the monotone illustrations.

D3: England: Drummer, Regiment of Foot, 1704
Information about drummers' uniforms in the British infantry at this period is very rare except that the customary practice of later years of dressing them in 'reversed' colours, i.e. with coats of the facing colour, lined and faced with red,

seems already to have been in existence. This figure is based on the description of a deserter from Lord Lucas's Regiment (later 34th Foot, Border Regiment), which was then faced with light grey. Lord Lucas's crest of the griffin and coronet was embroidered on the back of the coat and is also painted on the drum. This regiment spent most of the war in Spain, not joining the Flanders army until 1710, by which time Lucas had died and his crest may have been superseded by the new colonel's.

E1: Prussia: Grenadier, Regiment of Foot, 1709
This grenadier is of the Regiment of Alt-Dohna, which fought at Oudenarde and Malplaquet. It is curious that, with the coat lined red, the cuffs are blue, but it is shown thus by Knötel. His grenade pouch is black with the flap edged in red. A smaller cartouch box was carried by the musketeers of the regiment, who wore the universal felt hat bound with yellow lace. Officers had a gold-laced hat with a black feather within the brim, and blue lapels with gold lace loops buttoned back to just above the waist, where the coat was closed by two gilt buttons, also with loops. Similar loops and lace edging decorated the pocket flaps and cuffs. A silver sash went round the waist, and black stockings were worn with white garters. Company officers carried a spontoon and sword and wore a gorget round the neck.

E2: England: Ensign, Regiment of Foot, 1708
During William III's reign the number of colours in the English and Scottish Foot, other than the Guards, was reduced from one per company to three per regiment. By the time of Marlborough's campaigns they had generally been further reduced to two: the colonel's, of a pure, plain colour, chosen by him but not necessarily matching the regimental facings, and emblazoned with some device, also usually of his choosing; and the lieutenant-colonel's, whose basic motif was the St George's Cross. After the Act of Union the St Andrew's Cross, a white saltire on a blue field, was added to the St George's Cross on the lieutenant-colonel's colour, and a similar, small 'Union' was added to the upper corner of the colonel's, nearest the pike. Before the Union Scottish lieutenant-colonels' colours naturally

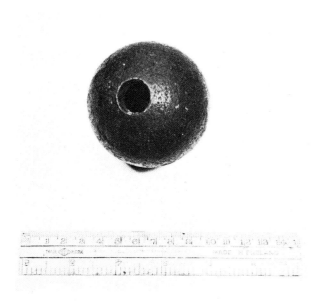

A hand grenade, *c*.1690. (H.M. Tower of London)

had the St Andrew's not the St George's Cross. The colour shown here is one, probably the lieutenant-colonel's, known to have been taken from the Buffs at Malplaquet. It still shows the Royal Cypher of the previous reign, William and Mary, with a coronet and flame above but with the St Andrew's Cross added after 1707. The Buffs, or Duke of Argyll's as they were officially known after 1707, formerly General Charles Churchill's, had, unlike some regiments which changed their facings according to their colonel's whims, consistently worn buff, or 'flesh-coloured' as it was sometimes described, since they were taken on to the English establishment in 1665 as the Holland Regiment. The ensign here has buff cuffs, although they were just as likely to have been red, as explained in D1. There is no evidence to show that officers of the Buffs had silver lace uniformly at this date, though they definitely did so by the reign of George II. The lace had no bearing on the rank held, this being indicated by the gorget, which was ordered in 1684 to be gilt for captains, black with gilt studs for lieutenants and silver for ensigns; it bore the Royal Arms. Since he carries a colour this ensign has dispensed with his pike or spontoon and is armed only with a sword.

E3: Hanover: Trooper, Regiment of Dragoons, 1708
Although the Hanoverian infantry wore red

coats, the Elector's cavalry were dressed in white with regimental facings, the blue shown here belonging to von Bülow's Regiment, which fought at Oudenarde. The skirts of the buff waistcoat, which was edged with blue lace, were turned back, as were the skirts of the coat—a fashion soon to be adopted by all armies. At the turn of the century the regiment had worn white hats but later changed to the more common black. The officers' hats were gold-laced and their coats had blue lapels turned back with gilt buttons and gold lace loops, which also decorated the button-holes on the cuffs and pocket flaps. They wore a yellow sash over the right shoulder.

F1: Prussia: Fifer, Foot Guards, 1704
Although all the Prussian infantry wore dark blue, only this regiment, the 'Füsilier-Leibgarde', had white facings. The parti-coloured lace was peculiar to its drummers and fifers. The ordinary rank and file wore the same cap but a plainer coat, lined and faced with white, with the same small collar as in E1 but white, and the same narrow, plain white lace loops on the button-holes of coat and waistcoat that can be seen on the fifer. They wore their coats open, like the grenadier in E1, with the waistbelt over the waistcoat. Their pouches, suspended over the left shoulder, had a black flap, edged with yellow, yellow grenades in the corner and in the centre the Royal Cypher, 'F.R.' (as on the cap), in yellow within a yellow circle. The 'Füsilier-Leibgarde' took part in the siege of Lille in 1708 and fought at Malplaquet.

F2: Austria: Trooper, Regiment of Hussars, 1709
Austrian hussar costume derived from Hungarian national dress and the origins of the familiar hussar dress worn later in all armies can be seen here: the fur cap with bag, the short jacket or dolman fastened by cords with buttons or toggles, the barrel sash, originally a picketing rope, the sabretache, originally a container for the man's belongings, and the short boots. Their hair was plaited and weighted with lead to fall over each ear as a rudimentary protection against sword cuts.

F3: England: Sentinel, Regiment of Foot, 1709
This figure shows the backbone of Marlborough's

Marlborough with his army crossing the Lines of *Ne Plus Ultra* at Arleux, with Bouchain in the background. Detail from a tapestry by De Vos at Blenheim Palace. (The Duke of Marlborough)

army, the ordinary soldier, or 'centinell' as they were then called, of the English Foot. It is based on the list of clothing and 'other necessarys' in 1709 for General Erle's Regiment (later 19th Foot, Green Howards), which at this time had yellow facings. The regiment joined the army in Flanders in time for Malplaquet and the remaining campaigns of the war. While the corporals' and sentinels' coats were of red cloth, the former's being of better quality, the sergeants' were crimson with silver lace on the seams and on their hats. Broad and narrow lace was provided for the coats of the 74 grenadiers in sufficient quantity to lace all the seams and provide loops for the button-holes, possibly on the waistcoat as well. The three grenadier sergeants' caps cost eighteen shillings each as opposed to the four and sixpence for the rank and file caps, so must have had gold or silver embroidery on them. The sentinel's felt hat cost only half a crown. The grenadiers therefore were more ornately and expensively dressed than the other companies. The 26 drummers had

'reversed' coats with lace, which also decorated their belts and drum carriages (as in D3) and 'worsted badges and cyphers', probably sewn on their backs. The regiment had a drum-major, whose yellow coat was embellished with both silver and black lace, while his badge and cypher were gold and silver. The design of this badge is not given, but as the yellow and black derive from the arms of the former colonel, Luttrell—'or, a bend between six martlets sable'—this design may have been retained under Erle. The sentinel here has a red waistcoat, made from the previous year's coat, but as the coats were lined with yellow the waistcoat too might have been yellow to match the breeches. Apart from his waistbelt and pouch-belt slung over the left shoulder, he carries his knapsack over the right. In addition, a proportion of the men carried their cooking pots on the march, as can be seen in the Oudenarde tapestry.

G1: Holland: Officer of Artillery, 1705
As was the case with the artillery of most armies, uniforms were generally more utilitarian than in other arms of the service. Apart from the gold lace round the cuffs, this Dutch officer's coat is very plain, though a fashionable note appears in his red heels. In contrast, a portrait of the English Master-Gunner, Colonel Pendlebury, shows a scarlet coat and waistcoat both richly embroidered in gold, an altogether more expensive costume. An all-blue coat was worn by the Prussian artillery with buff waistcoat and breeches, while the Austrian gunners were dressed completely in grey, relieved only by dark red cuffs (see monotone illustrations).

G2: England: Trooper, Regiment of Horse, 1709
This figure shows the uniform of Cadogan's Horse and is based on the description of a deserter: 'Hat with Silver Lace, red Regimental Coat faced with Green, and broad silver Lace on the Sleeves, and Sleeves and Pockets bound with narrow [lace], green Wastecoat and green Shag [worsted with a velvet nap] Breeches.' The same notice mentions the hair being tied in a black bag, a practice then becoming common, which can be observed both in the tapestries and the Laguerre paintings. The breast plate reintroduced for the English Horse in 1707 can be seen under the coat. The trooper is armed with a sword suspended from the right shoulder-belt, two pistols in holsters on the saddle, and a carbine attached to the left shoulder-belt.

G3: England: Gunner, Train of Artillery, 1709
The men of the Train included gunners, who charged, laid and fired the gun, matrosses who assisted them with tasks around the gun position, pioneers, pontoneers and artificers. The drivers and waggoners were all impressed civilians. The coats of the Train are variously described as crimson, red and scarlet, lined and faced with blue, sergeants usually having the former. The description of a matross in 1708 gives his coat as lined with black, black buttons and lace loops, black waistcoat and red breeches. The yellow worsted lace of this gunner's scarlet coat, worn also by pontoneers,

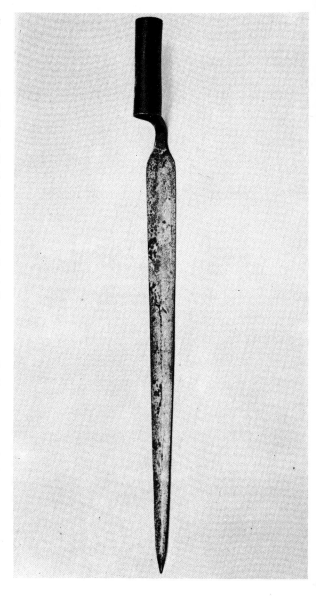

Socket bayonet, c. 1710. (Central Library and Cuming Museum)

would be gold for NCOs. Matrosses and pioneers had red coats. He has a powder horn slung over his left shoulder and carries a linstock.

H1: Prussia: Officer, Foot Guards, 1702
Although Prussian guardsmen wore blue turned up with white (see F1), their officers had red coats and waistcoats with black breeches and stockings, continuing the prevalent 17th-century practice of officers dressing differently from their men. This was soon to die out as greater uniformity

was striven for. The contemporary print on which this figure is based is dated 1700, when Prussia was still Brandenburg, but the Guards officers' red coats were still being worn after the Electorate became a kingdom. He is armed with a partisan and a sword.

H2: England: Corporal, Regiment of Dragoons, 1704
This figure is based on various descriptions of the Royal Scots Dragoons from 1687 when they adopted red coats faced blue instead of the grey worn formerly. The yellow lace loops on a corporal's coat are speculative, though they definitely appeared on a sergeant's. The broad gold lace on the cuff to indicate corporal's rank is taken from a clothing list of the Royal Dragoons. Their sergeants had additional gold lace on the sleeves, pocket flaps and waistbelts. This dragoon carries a musket and bayonet as well as his sword. The hatchet, hanging from a frog behind the pouch, was used for clearing obstacles in advance of an army or chopping timber to make fascines for filling in ditches or trenches. The Scots Dragoons' use of grey horses is recorded as early as 1694, and in the Donauworth (or Schellenberg) tapestry a regiment on light-coloured horses can be seen advancing with fascines across their saddles. In his hat this corporal wears a bunch of straw, the field sign of the Allied armies in this action.

H3: Holland: Trooper, Regiment of Cuirassiers, 1708
This figure is taken from a contemporary picture of Oudenarde by Huchtenberg. Cuirassiers of different armies bore a similar appearance to one another and this trooper wears the Allied field sign for Oudenarde of green leaves. Unlike the Austrian cuirassier (D2) he wears a hat, probably with a metal skull inside, and a grey cloth coat, faced red, instead of the buff leather. His weapons and accoutrements are similar. The red holster covers and housing may have had additional devices or edging, but the details of the original picture are too imprecise to make these out.

'In Flanders. A market tent in Camp'. The drinking and dancing soldier at right appears to be an Austrian hussar. Drawing by Marcellus Laroon. (Courtauld Institute of Art)

Notes sur les planches en couleur

A1 Costume provenant des tapisseries de Blenheim Palace exécutées sous la surveillance du Duc lui-même et que nous supposons donc exactes. La quantité de galons dorés de la redingote variait de temps en temps et nous illustrons ici la version portée à Donauwörth. Le ruban de l'Ordre de la Jarretière se porte sous la redingote. L'épée et la couverture de selle sont tirées d'objets conservés. **A2** Le portrait par van Schuppen montre Eugène portant un casque burgonet mais à part cela nous l'avons fidèlement suivi pour cette illustration. La redingote à galons bruns et dorés n'avait pas les grandes manchettes de l'époque. L'Ordre de la Toison d'Or se porte sous la cuirasse. **A3** En sa qualité de Commandant de l'Armée, le Duc de Marlborough avait deux trompettes d'état à son service. Remarquer les fausses manches qui retombent au dos de la veste. En 1705 à Elixem un des trompettes sauva le Duc de Marlborough d'un cuirassier bavarois géant.

B1 Remarquer l'insigne aux chardons portée sur le devant du bonnet. A partir de 1712 le régiment avait des manchettes bleues. Cette redingote n'a pas les galons d'argent portés parfois par les sergents et la hallebarde est la seule indication du rang. **B2** La plupart des troupes hollandaises et d'autres pays portaient des redingotes grises d'où les écharpes de couleur et les 'insignes de bataille' comme par exemple ici la brindille feuillue au chapeau afin de permettre d'identifier rapidement les soldats. Vous remarquerez au pied du soldat le bonnet commun de grenadier de l'infanterie hollandaise. **B3** L'infanterie danoise portait des parements de couleur différente à ses redingotes grises pour identifier les régiments.

C1 Nous avons tiré cet uniforme de la peinture de Blenheim par Laguerre et de la tapisserie de Blenheim. **C2** Contrairement aux redingotes grises habituelles de l'infanterie autrichienne, les sept régiments Wallons portaient des redingotes vertes à parements pourpres. Les officiers grenadiers portaient le chapeau au lieu du bonnet des soldats et avaient un mousquet léger. **C3** Les gardes à pied hollandais se distinguaient par des uniformes bleus et oranges; remarquer les longues manches du gilet visibles sous les manchettes du manteau.

D1 Le goût personnel de chaque officier dictait la quantité et le motif des galons dorés ou argentés portés sur la redingote et généralement ils ne portaient pas de parements assortis à ceux des hommes de leurs régiments. **D2** Au début du 18ème siècle les cuirassiers autrichiens avaient toujours le manteau en peau de buffle, le casque et la cuirasse, rappelant la Guerre de Trente Ans. **D3** Basé sur une description d'un trompette du régiment de Lord Lucas (plus tard le 34ème régiment d'infanterie). On remarquait déjà certains trompettes portant des redingotes aux couleurs inversées comme elles se feront plus tard.

E1 Nous tirons ce costume d'une peinture du Régiment Alt-Dohna par Knötel qui se battit à Oudenarde et à Malplaquet. **E2** Les couleurs du second ou du Lieutenant-Colonel du régiment du Duc d'Argyll—les célèbres 'Buffs', plus tard le 3ème d'infanterie; remarquer l'enseigne toujours au chiffre royal de Guillaume et Marie. **E3** Les parements bleus identifient le régiment de van Bülow qui se battit à Oudenarde.

F1 Les parements blancs identifient le régiment des Füsilier-Leibgarde; les galons et passepoils multicolores n'étaient portés que par les trompettes et les joueurs de fifre. **F2** La naissance de l'uniforme de hussard dérivé du costume national hongrois. **F3** Fantassin anglais caractéristique, le pivot de l'armée du Duc de Marlborough; il s'agit ici du régiment du Général Erle, plus tard le 19ème d'infanterie, les Green Howards. Le gilet est rouge et la culotte est jaune.

G1 Uniforme simple typique de l'artillerie, rehaussé par le galon doré de la manchette et le talon rouge de la chaussure. **G2** Troupier de Cadogan's Horse avec parements verts, galon d'argent et cheveux serrés dans une résille noire—une coutume ordinaire. Remarquer la cuirasse portée sous la redingote. **G3** Le boutefeu est entouré d'une longueur de mèche et le soldat porte un cornet à poudre.

H1 Bien que les gardes prusses aient porté du bleu à parements blancs, les officiers portaient le rouge avec culotte et bas noirs. **H2** Le galon doré sur la manchette indique le rang de caporal; il s'agit ici du régiment des Dragons Ecossais Royaux. La paille au chapeau était l'insigne de bataille à Donauwörth. Ce soldat porte un mousquet et une baïonnette ainsi qu'un sabre et une hachette. **H3** Tiré d'une peinture contemporaine de la bataille de Oudenarde; les feuilles vertes au chapeau étaient l'insigne de bataille de Oudenarde. Ce soldat porte probablement un couvre-chef métallique de protection sous le chapeau.

Farbtafeln

A1 Die Kleidung ist nach den Wandteppichen zu Blenheim Palace abgebildet worden, diese wurden unter Aufsicht des Herzogs gewoben und sind, also, vermutlich getreu. Von Zeit zu Zeit hat sich die Menge Goldtresse am Waffenrock geändert—hier wird abgebildet wie er zu Donauwörth getragen wurde. Der Band des *Order of the Garter* wird unter dem Waffenrock getragen. Schwert und Schabracke sind nach überbleibenden Exemplaren abgebildet worden. **A2** Das van Schuppen Porträt vom Prinzen Eugen stellt ihn im *burgonet*-Helme dar: in anderen Einzelheiten stellen wir ihn nach diesem Bildnis dar. An der braunen, mit Goldtresse geschmückten Jacke fehlten die tiefen Ärmelaufschläge der Periode. Über dem Kürass wird der Goldvliesorden getragen. **A3** Als Heereskommandeur standen zwei Staatstrompeter dem Herzogen von Marlborough zur Verfügung. Bemerkenswert sind die 'Scheinärmel', die hinten an der Jacke hängen. Im Jahre 1705 zu Elixem hat ein Trompeter den Marlborough von einem riesigen bayrischen Kürassier gerettet.

B1 Zu bemerken ist das Distelemblem vorne an der Mütze. Ab 1712 hat das Regiment blaue Ärmelaufschläge getragen. An der Uniform fehlt die von dem Feldwebeln manchmal getragene Silbertresse und die Hellebarde bietet das einzige Dienstgradkennzeichen dar. **B2** Die meisten holländischen Truppen und die vieler anderer Nationen trugen graue Waffenröcke: für rasche Erkennung, also, waren färbige Leibbinden und 'Feldzeichen' wie ein Blätterzweig am Hut nötig. Zu seinen Füssen liegt eine wie von dem gemeinen Soldaten getragene Grenadiersmütze. **B3** Bei der dänischen Infanterie sind die Regimente durch die verschiedenen Farben der Aufschläge ihrer grauen Waffenröcke erkannt worden.

C1 Diese Uniform ist nach dem Laguerre Bild von Blenheim und von dem Blenheimer Wandteppich abgebildet worden. **C2** Im Gegensatz zu den grauen Waffenröcken der oesterreichischen Infanterie trugen die sieben wallonischen Regimente im allgemeinen grüne Waffenröcke mit hochroten Aufschlägen. Grenadieroffiziere waren mit Hüter anstatt der Soldatenmütze ausgestattet und tragen eine leichte Flinte. **C3** Die holländische Fussgarde war durch blau/orangegelbe Uniforme gekennzeichnet. Bemerkenswert sind die langen Westenärmel, die unter den Ärmelaufschlägen der Jacke sichtbar sind.

D1 Die Menge und das Muster der Gold/Silbertresse auf Offizierswaffenröcken war vom persönlichen Geschmack abhängig und normalerweise haben die Offiziere mit ihren Regimenten eingestimmten Aufschläge nicht getragen. **D2** Am Anfang des 18. Jahrhunderts haben die oesterreichischen Kürassiers immer noch wie im 30 Jährigen Kriege Röcke, Kürasse und Helme aus Büffelleder getragen. **D3** Nach der Beschreibung eines Trommelschlägers im Regimente des Lord Lucas (später das 34. Infanterieregiment) abgebildet. Die spätere Gewohnheit für Trommelschläger Röcke in 'umgekehrten' Farben zu tragen kam zu dieser Zeit schon manchmal vor.

E1 Diese Figur ist nach einem Bild von Knötel des Regiment Alt-Dohna, das bei Oudenarde und Malplaquet gekämpft hat abgebildet worden. **E2** Die zweite, oder 'Oberstleutnantsfahne' des Duke of Argyll's Regiment—die berühmten Buffs, später das 3. Infanterieregiment: das königliche Monogramm von Wilhelm und Marie steht noch heutzutage auf dieser Fahne. **E3** Durch die blauen Aufschlägen erkennt man das von Bülow Regiment, das bei Oudenarde gekämpft hat.

F1 Durch die weissen Aufschläge wird das Füsilier-Leibgarderegiment erkannt; bunte Tresse und Schnurbesatz wurden nur von Trommelschlägern und Querpfeifenspielern getragen. **F2** Hier kann man die Ursprünge der von der ungarischen Nationaltracht abstammenden Husarenuniform erkennen. **F3** Der typische britische Infanteriesoldat, die Stärke von Marlboroughs Armee; das heir geschilderte Regiment ist das von General Erle, das spätere 19. Infanterieregiment, The Green Howards. Rote Weste, gelbe Kniehosen.

G1 Typisch einfache Artillerieuniform, hier durch die Goldtresse an den Ärmelaufschlägen und die roten Absätze der Schuhe belebt. **G2** Reiter von Cadogan's Horse: grüne Aufschläge, Silbertresse und Haare—wie allgemein üblich—in einem schwarzen Beutel gebunden. Zu bemerken ist das unter dem Waffenrock getragene Kürass. **G3** Um den *linstock* ist eine Länge Zündschnur gebunden worden und der Soldat trägt ein Pulverhorn.

H1 Obgleich die Soldaten der preussischen Garde blaue Uniforme mit weissen Aufschlägen getragen haben, trugen die Offiziere rote Waffenröcke mit schwarzen Kniehosen und Strümpfen. **H2** Gefreitendienstgrad ist durch Goldtresse an den Ärmelaufschlägen gekennzeichnet: das Regiment, the Royal Scots Dragoons. Der am Hut befestigte Strohalm war das 'Feldzeichen' zu Donauwörth. Flinte und Bajonett trägt er sowohl als Schwert und Beil. **H3** Von einer zeitgenossischen Abbildung von Oudenarde; bei dieser Schlacht waren grüne Blätter am Hute das 'Feldzeichen'. Höchstwahrscheinlich wurde ein Kopfschutz aus Metall unter dem Hut getragen.